so you want to be in music!

FOREWORD

About a year ago I learned that Jesse Burt and Bob Ferguson were writing a book about the music business, writing for amateurs who want to become professionals. Bob and Jesse worked hard and long and now the book exists.

I have read their book, and I like its content. It is positive, for one thing, but it is realistic, too, because there's an awful lot of misconception about this business.

Here and there, some points might be stated differently, but that is true of any book. This is a simple, factual, interesting handbook for the amateur who is serious about getting into the music business.

At the same time, the authors are rendering a needed service to the honest people in the recording business.

Chet Atkins

PREFACE

Nearly every professional in the music business is asked questions like these:

"Are my songs any good?"
"What really happens in a recording studio?"
"How much do you make from a million-seller song?"
"What are studio musicians paid?"
"Are there any nonperforming careers in the music business?"

In this simplified handbook we will examine and explore questions like these as well as hundreds of others that amateurs often raise. The book is for those everywhere who want to pursue careers in the business of creating, performing, and recording popular music. It applies, in general, to all of the major centers of music production; New York, Hollywood, Toronto, Nashville, and elsewhere. As one New York consultant wrote: "The principles of making it in music are essentially the same, regardless of geography."

Evidence collected from music publishers, recording companies, songwriters, performers, juvenile courts, and Traveler's Aid indicates that many, if not most, of those seeking to try out in music lack essential background information. They arrive in one of the major recording centers unprepared. This handbook presents the kind of practical facts and advice they can understand and apply.

As you look over the table of contents, you will see that we start with the general in order to consider the specifics. We take a broad look at the music business as it really is. It is this setting that is provided in the first part of the book.

SO YOU WANT TO BE IN MUSIC!

Against this setting, aspects are presented which take you gradually into the business. This is developed in Part Two. The third part presents detailed information and specific ground rules pertinent to commercial songwriting. Part Four examines existing career opportunities in recording and associated, or supporting, branches of the business.

Our primary goal is to help stimulate clear thinking, constructive self-examination, realistic planning, and efficient follow-through. Another goal is to alert you to the scarcity of time and the need to manage the time you have. Further, we wish to state frankly the pitfalls and fallacies that may confront you as you get started. The bitter as well as the sweet will be brought out. The final goal is quite honest: if you can contribute to the music business, be successful in it, the authors will be gratified.

There is an old saying, "If you would understand an Indian, follow in his moccasin tracks." You may have the talent, knack, or business head to follow in the tracks of those who have organized and built the music business. You may, in your stride, contribute to its further development. This handbook will help you find out if the music business is for you.

Jesse Burt

Bob Ferguson

ACKNOWLEDGMENTS

It would be impossible to list all the individuals, groups of individuals, and organizations who have befriended this research, writing, and publishing project. In many instances, for example, the staffs of individuals reviewed the preliminary outline of this book. Notwithstanding our limitations, we acknowledge, insofar as we can, the generous aid received.

Chester Atkins and Ronald Spores read the entire manuscript in its third complete revision; also Jim Atkins.

Among those reacting to the preliminary outline: Peter Sayers; Susan Sutton; Allen Pettus; Jim Andrews; Peter Small; Marion S. Egbert; Hubert Long; Bill Anderson; Moneen Carpenter; Bud Brown; Dorothy Horstman; Marge Parker; Cy Coben; Brad McCuen; Ed Shea; Donna McClurkan; Eleanor Burt; Gene Rowe; Judy Kinnard; Ruth Kinnard; Danny Davis; Tandy Rice, Jr.; Mike Weesner; Ken Winston, Jr.; Ken Thompson; Fred Cloud.

Among those reacting to the handbook's general concept or to some specific concept in it, or both: Bernie Schweid; Mrs. Henry Cannon (Minnie Pearl); Norro Wilson; John D. Loudermilk; Billy Edd Wheeler; Bill Anderson; Tex Ritter; Chet Atkins; Frances Preston; Mary Lynch Jarvis; Felton Jarvis; Bill Williams; Shirley Mayo; personnel of the Marty Robbins office; Connie Smith; Dorothy Gable; Jo Walker.

Reviewers of particular chapters or entire portions of the book: Brad McCuen; Joe Talbot; Lawton Williams; Mickey Newbury; Cal Everhart; E. J. Hines; Dorothy Boyd; Junior Huskey; Jimmie Peppers.

SO YOU WANT TO BE IN MUSIC!

For special helps, or unpublished insights, or both: Emily Bradshaw; Claude (Curly) Putman, Jr.; Harlan Howard; Don Davis; Jerry Green; Ralph Emery; Boyce Hawkins; George Hamilton IV; Jerry Reed; staff of WSIX-TV; Charlotte Tucker, and others at Acuff-Rose; Bob McCluskey; Merle Travis; Carl Smith; Ernie Ashworth; Penny Lane; Dottie West; Bill Crawford; Wendy Dawn; Audie Ashworth; Kelso Herston; Betty Siegfried; X. Cosse; Roy Shockley; Jimmy Gately; Skeeter Davis; staff of Tree, International; Eddie Miller; Jake Hess; Ott Devine; Hank Mills; Stringbean; Helen Carter; Johnny Cash; Buffy Sainte-Marie; Merle Kilgore; Hugh X. Lewis; Billy Walker; Ferlin Husky; Bee Nelson; Jean Moore; Linda Cole; Juanita Jones; Pat Richman; and Martha Ferguson.

CONTENTS

Part I Know What It Is; Know What You Want

    1. You're Right, It's a Big Business   17
    2. What It Takes to Be a Pro   22
    3. Personal Checklist   27

Part II Breaking into the Business

    4. Why Drop Out to Get In?   33
    5. The "Big Break" Fallacy   39
    6. How You Get Started   45
    7. *Dos* and *Don'ts*   51

Part III Songwriting

    8. Sharks and Other Predators   59
    9. "Are My Songs Any Good?"   65
    10. Copyrighting and Submitting Songs   70
    11. How Songs Are Selected for Recordings   82
    12. "What's in It for Me?"   87

Part IV Recording and Associated Careers

    13. So You Want to Make a Recording   95
    14. The "Big Label" Syndrome   105
    15. Economics of Recordings   111

16. What Happens in a Recording Studio	118
17. Studio Sidemen	129
18. Others Who Get the Work Out	139
Appendix	151
1. Questions the Professionals Don't Have Time to Answer	151
2. Glossary of Professional Terms	156
3. The "Nashville Shorthand"	163
Reading List	167
Index	171

PART I
KNOW WHAT IT IS; KNOW WHAT YOU WANT

I

You're Right, It's a Big Business

Big business, big art, big sound, big money—
That's recorded musical sound today and the growth potential is significant in this, one of the youngest of the big businesses. Recorded music is not yet as old as the space industry, and this means, generally speaking, that career options will continue to emerge for the person who is really prepared.

People everywhere are fascinated by the opportunities in recorded music. There probably are more professional musicians than you realize; the American Federation of Musicians in the United States and Canada has a membership of 250,000. To these add the many thousands belonging to the American Federation of Television and Radio Artists (AFTRA), American Society of Composers, Authors and Publishers (ASCAP), Broadcast Music, Incorporated (BMI), American Guild of Authors and Composers, National Academy of Recording Arts and Sciences (NARAS), and other groups. A grand total of 750,000 professionals involved in the many aspects of the recording business is a conservative estimate. Sesac, Inc., a privately owned performance rights licensing organization, is believed by experts to have a catalogue representing some 100 active publishers that contains

SO YOU WANT TO BE IN MUSIC!

over 150,000 musical compositions, written by thousands of writers. These rough and staggering statistics suggest the size of the music business and also the large numbers of persons active in it. In spite of its size, however, the industry is within reach of those who prepare themselves for it.

Recordings

Recording sales annually in the United States total more than one and a third billion dollars in retail prices. Add to that another billion for sound-reproducing equipment. In 1969, when a U.S. space vehicle first orbited the moon, the command pilot played back to this planet "Fly Me to the Moon." On earth, another complicated computer system, this one measuring royalties for the owners of the copyright, registered another digit.

Who consumes this huge output of recorded music? The U.S. consumes 57 percent of the world's total product; Europe takes 25 percent; Asia, 7 percent; Latin America, 4 percent; Africa, 2 percent; Australia and New Zealand, 3 percent; and Canada, 3 percent.

Foreign Distribution

Record companies in the United States are classified into two categories in foreign distribution methods. Large companies, such as Columbia and RCA, have foreign subsidiaries in several foreign nations, and have licensed distributors in others. Smaller companies, on the other hand, usually rely on foreign licensees.

Of course each of the major foreign countries has record companies. In England two of the largest worldwide record companies are EMI Records and the Decca Record Company, Ltd. ("British Decca"). EMI reportedly manufactures one out of every four recordings on earth.

YOU'RE RIGHT, IT'S A BIG BUSINESS

Still another international giant is N. V. Philips Phonographische Industrie of Holland, known more simply as "Philips," which owns subsidiaries in England, France, the United States, Germany, Australia, and South Africa.

West Germany's Deutsche Grammophon Gesellschaft (DGG) is probably one of the larger international companies. It is affiliated with Philips. Both are owned by electrical manufacturing companies in Holland and West Germany, respectively.

It's New

As you have read, recorded sound is relatively new. In 1887, Edison invented the phonograph; the first record disc and cylinder were invented ten years later. Radio was perfected in 1902, with AM, FM, and stereo coming later. The first long-playing (LP) recording was issued in 1948 and was a selection of military marches.

Since recorded music is so young, it yet is developing; new techniques for recording, new types of recordings, and new uses of them may be expected. We can also expect periodic changes in emphasis in the production and reproduction of music. In the early fifties there was a gradual—sometimes resisted—change from 78 rpm to 45 and 33 1/3. Tape battles for supremacy over the pressed disc. Both stereo and mono recordings have their proponents. Change, swift and sweeping, is the order of the day in the recorded music business.

Barriers Are Relative

As Joan Baez has said, this recording business is without absolute barriers. Ralph Emery, influential WSM disc jockey, is fond of saying that it doesn't matter, in making a recording, who your grandfather on your mother's side was. Ray

SO YOU WANT TO BE IN MUSIC!

Charles, José Feliciano, and Stevie Wonder found in recording a way of surmounting physical as well as social handicaps.

Much has been written about the polarizing and fragmenting of society in these times, but take this story as an encouraging contrast. During the filming of a Johnny Cash television show at WSM's Grand Ole Opry House in Nashville (the place that gave Nashville its original start as an important music center) the backstage area was filled with people who differed greatly from each other. There was Buffy Sainte-Marie, a lovely Cree Indian singer-composer. The Carter sisters, writers, originally singers of traditional folk song, hovered around tall Johnny Cash, himself part Cherokee Indian. There was a hard rock band from Los Angeles. Another young man picked an electric guitar, and was joined by a country musician from Chattanooga. Within moments they were playing, in a dazzling exchange, "Wildwood Flower," though verbal communication between them probably would have been difficult.

A tall, well-barbered man listened intently to the two guitarists improvising their way through the melody he had recorded a good many years before. Chet Atkins was backstage at the Opry House, having just come back from a concert in London.

Through music, all these people were communicating with each other and were responding to each other in a civilized way.

The same is true when Bob Ferguson supervises a recording session with Argentina's Palito Ortega. Ortega can speak no English, but communication is complete—through music.

Music Is Now

The hills and plains are alive with the sounds of recorded music. So are Mayfair, South Africa, Toronto, the ghetto.

YOU'RE RIGHT, IT'S A BIG BUSINESS

The beaches pulsate to it, from loudspeakers, car radios, and the little transistors of the teeny boppers. This music simply is everywhere; it bombards you. We live by it, march to it, make love to it, protest to it, shop to it, and are laid to rest with it—*recorded music!*

Music is now!

Who hasn't written a poem, thought of putting music to it?

Music, U.S.A.

The American Music Conference finds that there are 44,000,000 amateur musicians in the United States, millions of whom read and use music.

There also are over 4,000 AM radio stations and 2,000 FM stations. They require a constant supply of recordings in order to exist.

Car radios, home radios, and various types of reproducers of recorded sound in the United States reach a total of 300 million. The consumers who own these products demand a constant flow of new music. The demand is supplied by those professionals who know of the need, have trained themselves to fill it, and daily guide the flow of recorded music from pen to studio, to marketplace, and to consumer.

2

What It Takes to Be a Pro

Like our colleagues we get letters like this one from a girl we'll call Sally, who was a high school junior in Memphis, and who wrote in part:

Having read five of your articles in youth magazines on music, I'm taking the liberty of writing you about myself. I am seventeen, and I think I have a good voice. I know it would be an interesting way to go if I could become a professional singer and make recordings. I need to do some thinking about all of this, so would you go to the trouble of giving me a few general pointers? I might not like the professional life!

Trying to answer a Sally-like question is as difficult as trying to thread a length of cooked spaghetti through the eye of a needle. It takes intense, intelligent, purposeful effort to become a professional in any endeavor. Only after years of experience in playing and singing can you determine whether you have enough talent, and whether you want to do anything with it. It is all so speculative, even if you have signed a contract with a major publisher as a writer or with a major recording company as an artist.

Sally was advised to that effect. It was suggested that she visit recording studios, continue her formal education, and seek advice about her singing from persons competent to judge. The answer may well have been less than satisfactory but then experts have just so much time, and it's possible that the amateur really doesn't want to know the truth. He is only "wishing that it might come true." Note that Sally just *thought* she had a *good* voice. Observation has shown that most singers who make it as recording professionals know that they have excellent voices, plus knowing they have the diction and the projection required. How much do you know about your talent as a performer, a player, or a songwriter?

What a Pro Is

A professional, states Webster's Seventh Collegiate Dictionary, is one who conforms to the technical or ethical standards of a profession, or "one participating for gain or livelihood in any activity or field of endeavor often engaged in by amateurs."

For example, in music there are certain general and specific ethics, one of which requires that you avoid copying, however subtly, the work of someone else. Other standards can be learned only from being in the business.

Also, you have no right to call yourself a professional until you can fully support yourself through whatever it is you opt to do in recorded music. You are a semiprofessional if you need to supplement your earnings from other activities. You are a professional only when you are more proficient than the 44,000,000 amateurs who, in effect, are your competition in the United States. However, being a professional involves not just money. Far from it. Marion S. Egbert, vice-president of the American Music Conference, says: "The music profession is second to none for those who find their greatest enjoyment in the world of music—in performing it and sharing it with others."

This notion of sharing, or contributing, is one of the leading themes of this handbook; with variations, it will be heard from time to time. Do you perform for your enjoyment, or for the enjoyment of others?

A Constellation of Traits

Long research, discussion wtih experts, and many years of experience in the business permit this flat observation: the professional usually is characterized, rather than by just a single, shining characteristic, by a constellation of traits, all centering around his dedication to music.

Recently the Music Educators National Conference, of Washington, after surveying thousands of music teachers across the country, compiled a brief but pointed list of traits believed by teachers to be important for those hordes of students who want to follow the professional life in music. Though the compilation was not limited to sound recording, it will be helpful to you as you begin assessing what you have to contribute, and the traits you must develop to make your contribution a large one.

1. Ability to communicate
2. Ability to organize detail
3. Good health and good health habits
4. Adequate energy
5. Lively imagination

This list was submitted to an aspiring guitarist, who then exclaimed, "Great, just great! But wouldn't all these blessings work just fine in any profession?"

The guitarist unconsciously hit upon a guiding principle: yes, if you have the traits to succeed in commercial music, you probably could make a go of nearly any other commercial activity. The requirements of excellence in commercial music demand so many talents—all of them marketable—that the pros often excel in other fields.

WHAT IT TAKES TO BE A PRO

Other Traits

Traits of professionalism could be listed at length. For example, high intelligence that can be applied quickly is a fundamental expectation of the studio musician. A sideman (supporting player or singer) who comes up quickly with a fresh innovation or lick will be sought after by the major recording companies. Someone has said, "No licks, no work."

An adequate musical background is becoming important in commercial music. Roger Williams, who grosses over $1,000,000 annually from sales of recordings and various personal appearances, holds a doctorate in music; Ray Stevens is a university graduate who majored in music; and Bill Purcell has a master's degree.

The professional is a master of the art of selling himself, and one way to sell himself is to share his enjoyment of music with others.

A sanely realistic outlook is desirable. Chet Atkins has stated that as a professional musician he realizes he must continue to grow. This is no mean task, since Chet's albums are studied and copied by the growing number of buffs in his audience. He takes part in concerts, particularly with local symphonies, in order to challenge his determination to improve. Though he has been widely recognized as a master guitarist for over a quarter of a century, Chet now is taking lessons on the classical guitar.

A professional is objective about his relative preparation, realizes he is obliged to continue preparing. He establishes goals, achieves them, and then raises other goals.

Reminders

Some of our consultants wanted this book to make clear that booze and drugs and professional careers in the tightly

SO YOU WANT TO BE IN MUSIC!

disciplined recorded music scene are incompatible. Look at what George Shearing says: "I don't drink, smoke, or engage in dope, and I am a happy man who enjoys (for a traveller) a conventional life. This is not peculiar with me, for you will find that many of my colleagues in jazz, well-known to you, lead similar lives." [1]

The consultants also urged us to emphasize that the business is a realistic, hard-cold-facts-of-life endeavor. Wrote one: "If you can, remind them that no one sent for them." Said ace songwriter Harlan Howard, "Remind them that the next person arriving in the reception room may be able to do your thing, and do it better." Roger Williams, speaking to a young audience in Chicago, boiled the professional adventure down to one axiom that applies to your life: "Musical careers are tough, tough—no matter if they're arranging, composing, or performing. Drive is the important thing—you have to have the itch to get there and make it big." [2]

Summary

The pro we have been analyzing in the ideal and the abstract is sensitive but tough, not too temperamental (not a problem-maker), a businessman, not a bon vivant. He has a fine talent that is disciplined. He can stay around for years.

---

[1] *Career Opportunities in Music* (Chicago: American Music Conference, 1966, p. 41. This pamphlet is an excellent source on the general field of music.
[2] *Ibid.*, p. 44.

3

Personal Checklist

The following informal checklist gives specific categories of requirements generally believed important to anyone aspiring for a career in recorded music. No extreme claims are made for it, but it may stimulate you to think systematically about your level of preparation. It would be helpful to you if you would write out in your own language the reasons for each of your responses.

If you can honestly answer yes in, say, twenty-five of the following, you have much to build on. Lower scores may indicate that a music career is not for you.

1. Money is not my dominant aim in life.
2. I can produce under pressure and don't rattle easily.
3. I'm more interested in people than things.
4. I can tolerate periods of discouragement without letting them be detrimental to my work.
5. I enjoy working long and hard, and can do so steadily.
6. Right now, I practice an average of three hours a day, and show steady improvement. I have practiced as much as six hours a day without abnormal exhaustion afterwards.
7. I agree that I must share my music with others.
8. I have won more than a dozen amateur contests, or have placed in the top three.

SO YOU WANT TO BE IN MUSIC!

9. I can manage my money, time, and temper.
10. I can tolerate periods of boredom and inactivity.
11. Music teachers, friends, and others say that I have excellent talent.
12. I do not have to retire at the same time every night.
13. I do not have a drinking or narcotics problem.
14. I realize that recorded music is a business and can explain fully what this implies.
15. I can read music, I know about counterpoint, orchestration, harmony, and music history.
16. I have supporting skills, such as a technical facility, manual dexterity, etc.
17. My emotional and physical health is excellent.
18. I am photogenic; that is, I do not "freeze up" when being photographed by either a photographer or television cameraman.
19. I know how to "work" various kinds of microphones.
20. I am willing to work on a job during the workweek and on my music at night and on weekends.
21. I have a rudimentary understanding of copyright law.
22. I have read about acoustics and electronics and have visited a number of sound control boards in radio and television stations.
23. I have often performed for payment as a singer or player in public.
24. I know in general how a recording studio works, from having visited many of them.
25. I can write music as well as song lyrics.
26. I am dedicated to the goal of becoming a professional.
27. I am a careful listener.
28. If I enter the recorded music field, it will be for the long haul, and I expect to grow and develop as a person in it.
29. I can think realistically without becoming cynical.

PERSONAL CHECKLIST

30. I am a hard but fair competitor; competition doesn't get me down.
31. I enjoy classical music.
32. I am tolerant of other people's musical preferences, even though I may not respond to their choice of idioms.
33. I read various trade papers, such as *Billboard, Cash Box, Record World,* and *Variety,* and consumer publications such as *Country Song Roundup* and others.
34. I not only want to contribute, but know that I *must* contribute. In addition, I know I shall make it in music only through enormous, intelligent effort, and then only if I excel. I have thoroughly evaluated my musical preparation.

Commentary

This informal self-inventory could be expanded to infinity. Perhaps other questions will suggest themselves to you.

In the following pages other requirements—as well as the satisfactions—of careers in recorded music will be discussed.

PART II
BREAKING INTO THE BUSINESS

The following two chapters discuss two important issues that you may have thought about: dropping out (of school, or job, or marriage, or society) in order to have a fling in music; the one big break that many people think explains how to succeed "overnight" in this business. Two additional chapters in this part of the handbook offer information about how you can get started in the business. Specific things to do and to avoid are given. Together, the four chapters give ground rules for breaking into the business.

4

Why Drop Out to Get In?

If the sociology of recorded music ever is written, it surely will contain a lengthy chapter relating the misadventures of those hopefuls who drop everything in order to migrate to a music center expecting immediate success there. Sometimes these dropouts are high school students; sometimes they are older people who quit their jobs or run away from their marriages. The following case history concerns a high school combo.

The Redheaded Peckerwoods

Five young men in the eleventh grade in a Midwestern high school decided to "go professional." They called themselves The Redheaded Peckerwoods, and had been playing together for three or four years. For the past two years they had been playing for money; some weekends they earned $100 or more, though it often was difficult to collect the money.

In order to go professional the combo felt it necessary to drop out of school. Frankly, it was hard to play on weekends and get up Monday morning to go to classes; school was boring, anyway, especially when you were unprepared for classes. Without the distraction of school, the group felt, their full time could be given to music.

SO YOU WANT TO BE IN MUSIC!

Next the Peckerwoods spent $3,000 on amplifiers, and another $5,000 on costumes and a red Volkswagen bus. All this was purchased on credit.

Then they took to the road in earnest, playing at taverns and roadhouses; there was plenty of work—at low prices. The group saw no need of joining the musician's union, which meant of course that they played only nonunion jobs. It might have been tough to get in the union because they had a history of working nonunion establishments.

After about six months of full-time playing the Peckerwoods scrounged up $500 and used it to make a recording of one of their teen songs. They tried to promote and distribute the recording with the aid of their mothers, but it sold only 1,300 copies in the local area.

They sent tapes of their work to various publishers and recording companies, but the tapes were returned. Thinking that a live audition might swing a recording deal for them, the Peckerwoods drove all night to reach a major recording company. After waiting ten hours in the reception room, they finally managed to see a certain producer. He agreed to listen to a "little of your playing."

The A&R man listened briefly, then asked the Peckerwoods to stop; he looked tired and discouraged. He said, "I don't think we can do anything for you, but thank you for coming."

All at once the Peckerwoods were clamoring for his opinion of their work, although the A&R man evidently did not care to discuss so intimate and personal a subject. Finally, he did say, "Guys, I hate to say this to you, but you're playing teen stuff that's old. Nothing changes as rapidly as teen music, you know. Now if you will excuse me, I've got to get back to the studio."

All the way back home the Peckerwoods argued among themselves, but as one member said, "He was telling the truth. We are playing old stuff, and that's all we know to play. And we have to play all the time just to get the money to meet the payments on the equipment. We don't have a chance to learn new music. We're too busy playing what we know. I say let's drop it."

On this note the Peckerwoods split up and disappeared, but their nine months on the road had resulted in a debt of over $8,000. One of the young men returned to high school, graduated, and went to college. The other four took such jobs as were available to persons with an eleventh-grade education.

Commentary

The case history suggests that self-deception is easy. Probably the Peckerwoods first concocted the illusion that they were ready for the professional life from the approval of their peer groups, or other teens. More than likely, they had played for other teens, and had been rewarded with extraordinary applause; applause from teens can be deceptive. Sometimes teens will applaud other teens as a way of letting off steam, or just to signify to adults that they are there.

Paul Revere is regarded as a thoroughly prepared musician, at the top as a leader and writer. He says, "The majority of kids want to be entertained, and they'll be watching more than they'll be listening."

So the Peckerwoods were deceived about their proficiency. They could have learned about their ability much more easily.

Why Drop Out?

By dropping out of school the Peckerwoods threw away two years in which they at least had the chance to improve their musical knowledge and their playing ability. When they dropped out of school they automatically entered the work category, though they were in a poor bargaining position. After their failure as would-be professionals, they confronted one of the basic circumstances of life: what can you do if you lack a high school education?

Unless you have a self-destruct instinct, why drop out of school to have a fling in music?

General Dropping Out

As was said earlier, dropping out can include also departure from your job, your home, your marriage, or your community as you know it. Many think that songwriting provides a wonderful technique for getting away from it all (whatever "it" encompasses). But how does songwriting work in real life?

Let's say that you have been writing musical compositions (words and music) for four or five years, and have had five of your songs recorded. You are married, have a family, and hold down a job in the daytime.

For a long time you have been mulling over an idea, and one day the title of a song pops into your mind—"Another Way of Saying I Love You"—and it seems to you to be like the material Peggy Lee or Dean Martin record. After a great deal of thought you decide on Dean Martin; you send a tape of your song, accompanying yourself on a standard guitar, to the Martin organization.

After this, you start working on another song—a change of pace—with James Brown as the vague target. You know enough not to bore your friends with talk of having submitted a song to Dean Martin; the important principle isn't submitting, it's being accepted, unless you are a "talking writer" (one who talks endlessly about writing).

Let's suppose that "Another Way of Saying I Love You" does remarkably well for itself in the Martin organization and ultimately is glowingly endorsed by Mr. Martin's various

WHY DROP OUT TO GET IN?

helpers and functionaries. Let's further suppose that Dean Martin listens to your tape and likes it, though he agrees with all concerned that "it'll take a lot of work." In time "Another Way" is recorded by Dean Martin. It sells one million copies.

Are you in now? Can you drop the tiresome job that takes so much energy and time? Hardly. For one thing, it will be nine months before your royalties start arriving, due to accounting and collecting procedures. In the interval you and your family need food, shelter, and clothing.

After you have collected your royalties from the Martin recording, you will be $10,000 richer, with about that much more coming from radio and television and other performances. Some of your friends may kid you about "making a million from just one song," or even "making it from just a song." Some may ask why you stick to your job: why don't you move to Hollywood?

However, experience reveals these realities. First, it's deeply satisfying to write a million-copy seller. Second, your total royalties are a far cry from a million dollars; and they may, the year you receive them, put you in a higher tax bracket. Third, self-discipline should insist that you write another, better song. Fourth, the Martin organization has not sent for you; you know little about Hollywood; you are familiar with your community.

A Theory of Dropping Out

If the broad notion of dropping out includes a reaction in favor of some needed improvement or change as you construe it, music can provide a vehicle for you to express your feelings. Tom T. Hall's "Harper Valley PTA" indicted smugness and hypocrisy; Bob Dylan's bibliography includes a number of compositions that highlight basic issues in man's contemporary style of living.

SO YOU WANT TO BE IN MUSIC!

Here is a tentative theory, then. If you are concerned about the ways of man, why not attempt to write a song that is commercial yet filled with content and meaning? Through recorded music you can communicate with human beings everywhere. Recorded music, therefore, has fully as legitimate an appeal and claim to the best talent as law, medicine, architecture, or any other professional calling.

Summary

Dropping out is wasteful; it is needless; it is the opposite of planning and preparing in order to intelligently enter the business. The general theory of dropping out, though the idea is tempting at times, is based on an illusion.

5

The "Big Break" Fallacy

"All I need is just one big break, and I'll be in like Flynn."

Someone responded to this with: "If I've heard that once in the twenty-five years I've been in the business, I've heard that a thousand times. It's funny how so many people will cling to a myth and be hurt by it, instead of knowing how it works in life. Maybe the movies have something to do with it. You sit there for maybe 90 minutes and you see a person start as a nobody, but before the film is over, he or she is a *star*. Just 90 minutes!"

Sometimes pros—not pausing to think of the years of preparation they have put into their own careers—perpetuate the fallacy of the "big break." An interview—like the movie mentioned above—is very brief, and the artist of necessity hits only the high spots of his career. As he gives credit to this person or that event, it must sound to the listener as though success is the result of one or two big breaks.

Herbie, a Loser

Not long ago a rumpled middle-aged man told about his twenty-year effort to "sell myself to some big shot who will make things happen for me." This man we will call Herbie.

SO YOU WANT TO BE IN MUSIC!

Like so many others, Herbie thought he could write commercial songs. Asked if he had received any acceptances, Herbie said, "Sure. I've had ten songs recorded," but he was vague about "when." He laughed, "What I need is a big break, that's all."

Asked why he didn't submit his material through the mail rather than languish hour after hour in reception rooms, Herbie explained patiently, "I'm a great believer in the personal pitch. If I can just get in, I know I can sell myself, to Jack Stapp or somebody big like him."

As he talked on and on, Herbie claimed that he had tried Nashville, New York, Los Angeles, and Chicago. "I'm like the man in Hank Snow's song. I've been everywhere, man, I've been everywhere." He added, "I'm a salesman by profession. It's not hard to get jobs in various cities."

He insisted that he had been trying for twenty years to place his songs, and, as if to prove his point, he opened a plastic portfolio and pulled out a half-dozen, badly smeared lead sheets. "Look 'em over and tell me what you think," he said.

The songs were dreadful; melodies were lifted intact from the public domain; words were banal. The songs lacked structure, interest, and originality. Their ideas were commonplace, had been written a hundred time before by competent craftsmen.

As it turned out, however, Herbie did not persist in asking for an opinion of his songs; he was much more interested in talking about his incessant efforts to interest Dale Evans and Roy Rogers in his work and in telling about the time he encountered Ernest Tubb in a parking lot and pitched a song to him right then and there.

Would that Herbie were merely an isolated, extreme example of a problem-maker. Regrettably he is one of the fixtures of the business, albeit on the outskirts.

THE "BIG BREAK" FALLACY

Commentary

The Herbies make problems; for credulous amateurs, who may be exploited in various ways by them; for professionals, who may be resented by them; and for the business, which must tolerate them.

Is there such a thing as a big break that will make you an overnight success?

Some years ago Frank Sinatra, Jr., treated rather briskly by the press, gave an interview in which he candidly admitted that being the son of an illustrious singer had both hurt and helped him. In the preliminary stage of the game being "junior" at least helped in getting a hearing. But in the nitty-gritty of making and selling recordings, the junior was a drawback; he was expected to outdo his father.

Nancy Sinatra also has discussed the problem she had when she started out as a singer. The question was, "Can she sing, or is she just the daughter of the chairman of the board passing herself off as a singer?" Nancy finally registered by recording material that sharply differed from that chosen by her father, notably the country-flavored million-copy seller "Boots."

In both instances, for Frank Sinatra, Jr., and for Nancy Sinatra, there was a long apprenticeship *before* the consumers' acceptance. That also was true of the father, who sang for years with Tommy Dorsey and other bands before making his first big seller.

The belief that there is a big break has the appeal of magic, good luck, and, conceivably, getting-something-for-nothing. The expression "just a song," heard so often, is roughly similar. People who insist on believing in myths have lost the game before it starts. The music business operates on a buyer's market; there is no way to compel people to buy a recording. Thus there are no magic wands to wave, no "open sesame" formulas.

The Contrast

The contrast to the big-break idea is far healthier. As Ralph Emery once said, making a hit recording is a wonderfully democratic operation. Charlie Pride showed that when he entered the country and western field with impressive results. Hank Williams, Jr., son of a legendary giant, proved his right to be himself. Liz Anderson, a California housewife, for a long time wrote songs and made tapes of them, accompanying herself on a chord organ. No one had ever heard of her when her material started receiving acceptances. As a prominent composer told the authors, "They don't care who you are, what you look like, what you like to eat. What they care about is what you *write*. I know this is extreme, but why confuse the issue? Publishers want *songs*."

"A Series of Breaks"

Tex Ritter once explained that, in his judgment, a successful performer enjoys a "series of breaks" in his career and "one thing leads to another. It would be impossible to point to just one example of good fortune, or good timing, and say 'Right there was my big break.'"

What Tex was saying can be broken down approximately like this: The good song leads to the good recording, which brings you the good royalties and, possibly, a contract with a music publisher. If you choose a performing career, you know the importance of a recording. The Beatles, Bing Crosby, Elvis Presley, Herb Alpert, Tom Jones, and many others demonstrate that one outstanding recording leads to many other things.

Surely it is correct to say to you that a good recording isn't a happenstance. Rather it's the product of intensive

THE "BIG BREAK" FALLACY

preparation undergirded by knowledge of what the consumers may be expected to accept.

Only in the sense of being alert to every opportunity can you have something that can remotely be called a break. There may or may not be an entity known as luck; most professionals in this business prefer the concept of good timing.

Why do some persons apparently enjoy good timing and others do not? Some of the answer may lie in the assumption that you can cultivate a background that will make you more receptive to opportunity, regardless of how insignificant the opportunity may seem. Every minute qualifies as opportunity if used carefully. For instance, you may be working at a job that you do not enjoy and you know that you can make it in music. The job quite probably does not take much thinking on your part. You can do what you are required to do, but in the meantime make plans and prepare yourself by careful reading in your time off. Keep your thinking to yourself; let your thoughts mature.

If you have acquired the knowledge, you can tell when the time is right for you. Along with knowledge goes experience. Take Connie Smith, often cited as a big-break star, since her first recording session produced the giant seller, "Once a Day," and took Connie from kitchen to concerts. If you talk with Connie about her background, you quickly learn that she sang for years as an amateur in Ohio and that she is extremely well informed about the techniques of recording. Her preparation, like that of George Hamilton IV, extends to her personal records; she has a series of scrapbooks documenting her career from amateur to professional—a real professional, who recently sang to an outdoor audience of 80,000 people. Seemingly born to sing, she was, when she faced her first recording mike, as sidemen say, "ready to sing." The time was right. She was prepared.

Summary

The nonavailability of a "big break" system should greatly encourage your preparation. The business is exactly as Ralph Emery says; it's democratic. If you have what it takes, if you're prepared, if your attitude is right, you will find the doors opening softly into the exciting world of music.

6

How You Get Started

This chapter briefly reports on how you can get started either as a commercial songwriter, recording artist, a sideman or background vocalist, or as one following an associated career in recording. You will remember that planning and preparing are endorsed by this handbook as being essential to career development. In Part Three, the book looks closely at songwriting; the fourth part of the book reports on recording and associated careers in depth. In other words, this part of the book—Part Two—is a preliminary to much more specific information.

Your question may be "When do you know that you're ready to try to get started?"

As in other aspects of life, hard-and-fast statements can be extremely misleading, but the question is often asked. Without being dogmatic about it the American Music Conference thinks that when you're about eighteen, and have considerable satisfactory experience in playing or singing or both, and are serious about music, not just hobbying, you are "ready." [1] Of course, there are exceptions, both ways. Judy Garland sang "Over the Rainbow" in her early teens, but

[1] *Career Opportunities in Music.*

SO YOU WANT TO BE IN MUSIC!

Nancy Sinatra made "Boots" when she was nearer thirty than eighteen.

Non-Studio Workers

The business of recorded music offers a variety of traditional kinds of jobs for which you apply in the traditional way. You ask for application papers, fill them out, provide references, and then are interviewed. These jobs include receptionists, stenographers, secretaries, file clerks, mail clerks, and the like. It is said that pay and working conditions for jobs like these in recorded music and music publishing offices and associated businesses compare favorably with those in other fields of business.

A time-honored option is a job that you can hold as a bread-and-butter provider until there is an opening in music. Typically, these have been jobs in advertising, journalism, public relations, and even (for young men) the post office. However, holding down one job while pursuing the goal of another can be challenging. If you think you can do it, make an intelligent investigation of job opportunities within your own local community that relate in some way to music. Radio and television stations, music departments of public libraries, or music stores (including department stores) may have vacancies, in addition to those sources of employment given. It is advisable for you to start where you are rather than to migrate impulsively to a primary recording center. You can mail your tapes to Nashville or Los Angeles quite readily from your home community. The waiting game somehow goes easier on home cooking.

Specialized Careers

Other non-studio careers include legal and tax specialists, promoters, publicists, managers and agents, accountants,

HOW YOU GET STARTED

maintenance engineers, and others which we will explore later in this handbook. In this preliminary account it is only proper to suggest that these specialized careers generally evolve after much seasoning and, in some cases, formal preparation such as law school. In many of these careers age is no particular barrier. However, competition from persons just out of college probably will soon confront middle-aged people in careers relating to the recording business.

Songwriting

To quote one well-known writer, "How on earth did I get started writing? Man, I don't know!"

Another songwriter was similarly puzzled, and added this relevant thought, "I can't explain where my song ideas originate . . . something out of the past, a news story, something overheard, something read."

Tentatively, this much may be said: experience plus research discloses no particular evidence of set patterns for starting off as a songwriter. Said another composer, "I didn't wake up one morning and say to myself 'From now on you are a songwriter.'" Harlan Howard said that as a boy in and around Detroit he wrote verses and sang them as a hobby. In Harlan's case full-time songwriting *evolved*, as it has with so many other writers.

Many interviews reveal that commercial songwriting generally develops as an auxiliary interest, an early hobby, a concern with various kinds of writing, or a wish for self-expression. However, it may be possible in the future to take courses in commercial songwriting in colleges and universities; you may be able to prepare for a career as a songwriter in a systematic, formal manner. Courses would be comparable to modern college offerings in short story writing and journalism, for example.

SO YOU WANT TO BE IN MUSIC!

You are started, it would appear, when you write steadily and with increasing facility, when you know about the structure of commercial songs, how to revise material, and how to submit songs. One way to begin is to perform your songs in public. But take simple precautions. Keep extremely unique ideas to yourself. After all, the *idea* is the core of many songs and someone might use yours. Begin keeping spiral notebooks containing ideas and thoughts as John Loudermilk does. Learn the rudiments of copyright and find out through the suggested reading list where to find more information.

Sideman/Vocalist

If you have had considerable experience in playing and singing and you have proof that you excel, you may choose a career as one who, in a recording studio, helps to provide the background for the recording artist or star. In order to succeed you must be brilliantly well prepared—truly a master of your instrument—for in the great recording centers excellence is commonplace. A later chapter will report on the life of the sideman, his lucrative pay and working conditions, and how you might become a sideman.

Ken Winston

Ken Winston, able young editor of *Face-to-Face* magazine, provided us with this summary statement:

What about songwriters or musicians? Should they write, write, write and/or sing, sing, sing to best learn and develop their talents? Also, what about staying in one's hometown and singing and playing in a combo and writing music to develop one's skills. This might be the best advice for some, instead of encouraging them to head to Nashville, New York, or the West Coast. . . . Certainly

HOW YOU GET STARTED

liking music and having some talent in it comes before any recognition one might receive from the public. My usual philosophy on most things is that if you are "good" you will make it. That is, you will "know" when what you do is good enough for a national audience. This means, as far as I'm concerned, that one is better off if he doesn't try to force the issue of the bigtime, although, certainly, it is important to make one's talents known.

Commentary

The answer to Ken's questions is, of course, that one should thoroughly prepare oneself—not only in a favorite specialized part of the recorded music business, but also in as many aspects of it as possible. When you do enter the scene you will be talking, living, and working daily with real pros in such varied aspects as promotion, production, publishing, merchandising, management, publicity, etc. While you are polishing up your specialty, learn the language of the music world. Then when you join it, you will join as a member, not as an alien.

Learn at home; there are plenty of ways. Study recordings and printed songs carefully, watch talented performers on stage and on TV. Put yourself mentally into the role of an apprentice whose aim ultimately is being a master, and study the pros. Gradually you can branch out into local performances, talent contests, local radio shows. Approach each appearance, each activity, as an additional opportunity to learn. Be the willing apprentice. As Ken says, when you are really good, really ready, you will *know* it. By constant application to your self-apprenticed work, you will grow. Ultimately this steady growth will lead you at the right pace into the world of the top professional. You will find yourself in a position to really contribute. The demands upon your time, in fact, will begin to exceed your ability to fulfill them.

It is a good idea to set your goals down on paper and

look back at them from time to time. Often it will surprise you to note that you have made progress. Too often we deviate from our goals. Our path begins to wander or become unclear. Again, a glance at the original goals can lead you back to the right pathway while restoring your faith and conviction. Enter amateur contests and aim to win them. Pat Boone won an early Arthur Godfrey Talent Scout contest. Seek advice from music teachers about careers in music and how to get in them. Chet Atkins' father was an accomplished musician and music teacher. Both Chet and his brother Jim were grounded in music fundamentals at home.

Visit recording studios when you can and make a point of attending all performances by great talents in your community. Once, in Palatka, Florida, the Ferlin Husky Show found itself without a microphone. A young native eagerly stepped forward to help out, suggesting where one could be secured. Everyone on the show was impressed by the eagerness and sincere interest of the youth; no one was surprised when he made it into the top echelon of recording artists a few years later. But in those early days Johnny Tillotson was a willing apprentice.

7

Dos and Don'ts

You may wish to think carefully about the idea of "experience," and that you always learn from it. The truth is that one may or may not learn from experience. It is possible to learn to do something in an incorrect way. Then relearning to do it will be tedious.

A traditional country saying is, "When you learn it wrong, it's twice-harder learning it right." An old pioneer's motto was, "Be sure you're right—then go ahead."

It also has been said, far too simply, no doubt, "The only thing that history proves is that man learns nothing from history." Benjamin Franklin declared, "Experience is a grim school, but fools will learn in no other." A certain painter, employed in a department store in a major city, has a sign that he uses which states, "Wet paint, but you don't believe it."

Experience is never a surefire way of correctly learning how to achieve a goal; it takes too much time. Vicarious experience—such as is reported here—is safer for you; you can keep it at a distance. You can draw from the vast store of musical knowledge and profit from the experience of others. Many have given it dimension, and it can be your heritage if you choose the world of music. But you must approach and make it yours if you would share the abundance of pooled knowledge that is available to you.

Marshall McLuhan stated that knowledge removes all obstacles and simply by-passes problems and allows them to wilt into insignificance.

Do seek knowledge.

No Time on Your Hands

Music is a business that operates on the general principle of "so little time and so much to do." The aim always is, as one A&R man put it, "to do the best we can within the time available." Recording sessions are usually exactly three hours long. Each minute is carefully used.

The superstars excel in planning time expenditures, in doing two or three things at the same time—like signing letters and talking on the telephone simultaneously—and in getting the work out. Brevity of speech and writing is helpful, provided it isn't so extreme that it is confusing.

Suggestions: use the odds and ends of time, the ten or fifteen minutes that have no particular allocation; be punctual; give sufficient time to rest, recreation, and sensible outdoor exercise; avoid the talkers, or the losers.

Our steady emphasis on work and learning isn't intended to discourage you but rather to encourage you to gain a full understanding of the business. As Marion Egbert said, "You should not make your decision based on any glamorous impression gathered from a movie or television drama."

Look back at the case history of The Redheaded Peckerwoods, their troubles and woes at the bottom of the industry. Understand that, however arduous it is at the top, anything less is also a struggle and can even be sordid.

Without any nagging, but remembering that vanity lurks everywhere, answer this question honestly: "Are you truly a fine musician with promise to excel, or are you merely the best among your fellow students?" Unless you can answer

DOS AND DON'TS

the first part of the question in the affirmative, you probably should not try to be a musician who plays for a livelihood. Have the courage to yield if the evidence suggests that you think about a career in some field other than songwriting or performing in recording studios. If you still want to be on the scene, you may wish to turn to one or more of the interesting supporting careers.

If you go professional, go for the top. If you want to make recordings, desire only to make *hit* recordings, nothing less.

Things to Watch

1. Guard against exhausting yourself. In this business long hours, fast work under high pressure, and constant excitement are hazards.

2. Know what you are signing. Eddy Arnold suggests that beginners shy away from contracts that extend longer than one year. In some cases, however, this may be difficult to do. Seek competent assistance.

3. Learn how to bargain and negotiate. Insist that agreements be put into writing and signed before witnesses. Be specific. Ask questions until you understand what is expected of you.

4. Do not tie up large sums of money on equipment. It may be that The Rolling Stones have invested $1,000,000 in sound equipment. For the average high school combo, or country and western band to tie up $4,000 or $5,000 in elaborate equipment, as many of them do, must be rated as so much squandering of money.

5. Peter Sayers suggests that you would do well to know that you can't live on royalties from recordings at first, maybe never. Remember that royalties are slow in coming.

6. Peter adds, "Don't copy other people, create your own style. Watch trends but don't be governed by them."

7. Know what a musical composition is (words *and* music, or music). There is no such thing as a "song poem." Either it's a song or a poem. People often harbor the idea that publishers will put music to words. This rarely happens.

8. Plan for the long haul; this is your lifework. A well-prepared bio (biography) is worth what it will cost. It can say what you can't very well say about yourself.

9. Attend carefully to your relationship with your fans. As already emphasized, you should play or sing or write for as wide an audience as possible.

Discipline vs. Discouragement

As a sensitive person you will have bouts with discouragement. Sensitivity, however, should not be considered a weakness. Feelings of discouragement, therefore, will be normal to you. After all, you face tremendous competition; you must continuously prove yourself. Successes can swirl you to dizzying heights; failures drop you to the lowest depths. This business is full of ups and downs that no one can anticipate or explain. You may have to alter your image, your style of writing and singing. As one star said, "And add that you may have heard every promise known to man, with little follow-through. Would that there could be a pill to wipe out memories."

In these moments or intervals of normal depression fall back on your conditioning and discipline as a professional. John D. MacDonald, distinguished contemporary novelist, makes this helpful observation:

I cannot detect any ritualistic procedures in my work habits, nor can I detect any self-conscious desire on my part to play some kind of game by making all my habits seem terribly ordinary. I just think that most professionals in writing, composing, sculpting, acting, etc., etc. *are* professionals because at some point they

DOS AND DON'TS

realize that a certain orderliness which one imposes on the hours of the day is necessary if one is to free the maximum attention for the project at hand. Later along, you learn that much of the work you do is as good or better when you have done it feeling pooped, discouraged, juiceless, .as work which turned you on at the time you were doing it. Once you know this, then the temptation to break off because you don't happen to feel up to par is greatly reduced.[1]

Prove the truth in MacDonald's assertion—through regular effort.

Summary

The *dos* well done can eliminate the need for any *don'ts*, although no one is infallible. Do remember the importance of music in all its forms. The music department of the public schools of Evanston, Illinois, said this about music: "Man must feel as well as think; he must create as well as discover and learn." If you meet the requirements, think of recorded music as an opportunity for you to *contribute* to others.

---

[1] *The JDM Bibliophile,* No. 11 (Downey, Calif.: 1969), p. 14.

PART III
SONGWRITING

There are legions and legions of versifiers everywhere, and many of them aspire to the status of lyricist, or one whose poem has been "put to music." This, they think, will produce a song that will sell.

This must be one of the outstanding oversimplifications about the recording business. Yet far too many sincere and well-meaning people pay to have their poems put to music, though the resulting concoction inevitably fails to meet the requirements of legitimate music publishers.

The dictionary defines a song as "a short musical composition of words and music," and this for purposes of general discussion may suffice. Clearly implied is the idea that the words and music go together so as to form a composition which obviously is a far cry from the simple scheme of "putting words to music." Defining precisely what the ingredients of a commercial song are would be a hazardous enterprise. A commercial song is a musical composition that many people want to buy because in some way they identify with it. Trends in recordings come and go in a flash; standards of acceptability, or taste, alter; and society changes rapidly. All these circumstances influence the writing of songs that are publishable.

Whatever else is true of a first-class commercial song—the

only kind of song worthy of your attention if you want to become a professional—it at least has content and sound that appeal to many people. Far fewer people buy recordings than hear them. As has been noted, nearly all recorded sound is becoming greatly more complex, particularly in terms of technology, thus reflecting the overall society which inspires its production. A seemingly simple folk song often has been polished and repolished innumerable times. Some of Paul McCartney's compositions defy classification; they are avant-garde; but it has been said that art to be art is always avant-garde.

Currently anyway the old-fashioned Tin Pan Alley "June-spoon-moon" lyricizing is not in demand by publishers and recording firms, nor is the three- or four-chord melody of "Three Blind Mice." This is as much as can be said with any finality in an era that is enjoying the fine compositions of Canadian writers, San Francisco writers, Simon and Garfunkel, John Hartford, and others. Once you have learned the craft of writing, avoid discouragement: you may help shape the next trend.

This part of the handbook reports on basics you need to understand thoroughly. Magic formulas and facile *how-tos* are avoided. In fact, cautions about pitfalls are reported along with many realities about commercial songwriting. Specific ways for evaluating your material are given; an outline of steps to take in copyrighting and submitting your songs is given. Also discussed are how songs are selected for recording and the economics of professional songwriting.

8

Sharks and Other Predators

Fringe operators are referred to as "sharks" in the recording and publishing business. Many of them advertise, "We'll put your song poem to music." Others promise other services in their ads.

To judge from the great number of these advertisements in American, Canadian, and British publications, sharks must do a good business, for advertising is expensive. Here and there, there may be legitimate enterprisers in this line, but blatant appeal to the ego or vanity trade is always suspect.

Learn about these sharks in order to avoid them.[1]

The Giveaway

The song shark, like the vanity book publisher and the phony literary "agent," always gives himself away: he advertises for submissions and he promises to appraise them for a fee. On the other hand, legitimate publishers and recording companies have no need to huckster for material, nor do they charge you for looking or listening.

The sharks promise that they will "place" your stuff with

[1] Excellent information is given in the leaflet "What Every Songwriter Should Know," published and distributed without charge by The Country Music Association, Nashville, Tennessee.

major labels. This is how they do it. A major label in New York actually receives a bale of lead sheets—as many as 400 different songs—every three months from one shark. As a New York source reported, "They were addressed to no one in particular, but at least this shark could then claim he'd submitted them to ──── label."

They do so claim in their ads.

Noncritical Acceptance

On one of Doris Day's television shows she deliberately wrote a mediocre song poem and sent it off to a shark in order to teach her musically inclined TV son about sharks. Sure enough, there was a glowing letter of acceptance from the shark, with a tough contract requiring Doris to pay fifty or sixty dollars for getting her song poem set to music.

In other words, the critical processes are out of the picture in song-sharking, both by the shark and his victim. For fees ranging up to $200, or more, the shark will "accept" anything sent his way. If it is garbage, that is all right: real sharks thrive on garbage.

What You Get

After you have paid the fee, you will receive a few pieces of "sheet music"; yes, your poem will be set to music. The setting will be as mechanical in its sound as the term suggests. The melody probably will be an "old Number 3," or a tune taken from the public domain (songs for which the copyright has expired).

What this setting amounts to is approximately this: the melody may not be compatible with the lyric; the tune may be unsingable; the work as a whole will lack integrity. It may be as ludicrous as a love lyric set to the tune of "Old Joe Clark."

Nevertheless, many hopefuls, having obtained lead sheets,

then will submit them to publishers. Sometimes they booby-trap their submissions by including a few grains of talcum powder in the envelope, hoping to determine whether or not the publisher looks at the unsolicited material. Many major publishers maintain open-door policies, though at considerable expense and with scant findings of anything they can use. The same holds true for many recording companies. Steve Sholes once observed that in twenty years of listening to unsolicited tapes and demonstration records he found only one song that he could record!

What you get from the song shark is poorly prepared sheet music. Unless you just want to have such sheets on hand, your money might well be spent on something else. The industry joins the U.S. postal authorities, Better Business Bureaus, and various trade associations in condemning the practices of the shark, but he must be thriving, nonetheless. We say submit your material properly and professionally to professionals.

"A Recording"

Another shark will make a demonstration record of your song after he has set it to music. Evidence indicates that you can quickly spend $500 for an acetate recording of hack music performed by pickup musicians. Again, unless you just want to have a recording around the house, you could better invest the same sum of money in song folios to study, excellent recordings to analyze, and basic equipment such as a tape recorder, in order to get on with learning how to submit your material to publishers who want commercial songs.

The "Come-on"

Still another predator advertises like this, "I will evaluate your song material for a modest fee." That's right, the initial fee will be twenty dollars or so; but you will discover that this only covers a preliminary "evaluation." A more thorough evaluation will be made for fifty dollars. The really skilled come-on manipulators can extract hundreds of dollars from the naive and the noncritical, the wishful thinkers.

The Losers

A Los Angeles songwriter, whom we will call Sandy, has made it after ten years. She writes, "Tell them to avoid the losers and the hangers-on. After they learn how recording studios generally operate, they don't need to hang around them. In my case, years ago, I almost got into the wrong crowd, the losers who trail after the stars all too often. They were always going to do something for my songs, they promised. I almost gave up the dream altogether, thinking that everybody was rotten and deceitful. Tell them to avoid the talk writers, the promisers, the fringe that you find in any business. The only way to do it is to submit your material. Don't waste time talking about it with somebody who can only talk and do nothing."

If you are really sure of your material, go to a legitimate publisher and ask permission to submit a tape recording of your song. There is nothing to pay and literally nothing to lose. The experience will be invaluable in what it teaches you. You may get a contract.

The Flat Fee

Selling a musical composition for a flat fee can result in a painful reality. There are instances in which a struggling songwriter sold for fifty dollars a song that later sold a million copies. In a few reported cases songs have been *given away,* only to sell a million copies eventually.

In 1947, or so the well-established story goes, Pee Wee

King and Redd Stewart, of the Golden West Cowboys, were tempted to sell "The Tennessee Waltz" for the conventional fifty dollars (apparently the preferred offer). However, the late Fred Rose, who had just started in publishing with Roy Acuff, star of the Grand Ole Opry, asked King and Stewart to let Acuff-Rose publish the song on the standard royalty basis. The two went along with this offer. "Tennessee Waltz," subsequently became the first song after World War II to sell a million copies of sheet music, and of course was a million seller for pop singer Patti Page. Various versions have reached sales of 6,000,000 copies, reportedly.

This song figured prominently in the rise of the Acuff-Rose music complex, which in turn contributed to the ascent of Nashville as a recording center of prominence, with roots in the Grand Ole Opry and WSM radio. If the writers had lacked faith in Fred Rose, history might have been different for all concerned. The point for you, wherever you are, is this: deal only with people you have reason to believe are professionals.

There are times when fifty dollars cash is hard to turn down, but as the saying goes, "Never sell yourself short, for if you do, others will believe you." Acquire now an understanding of the business as a business.

Summary

In the natural world, predators devour the unwary, the unprepared, the eager, the curious, the gullible. In the civilized jungle, as P. T. Barnum insisted, the con man knows in advance that the "mark" expects something for nothing, or much for little effort. The song sharks know this; they also are attuned to vanity. Veteran music publisher Brad McCuen said, "It is a little sad to note the extent of man's vanity in connection with song composition. Men who have amassed huge fortunes through their acumen in finance, law, medicine, manufacturing, etc., are most often blind to their complete lack of ability in songwriting. They squander small fortunes chasing a musical butterfly they can never hope to catch." On the other hand, the professional route promises nothing; it asks nothing of you except that your work be excellent.

9

"Are My Songs Any Good?"

"Are my songs any good?"

The question may be a supplication, an imperative, a request for advice, and so on. Whatever provokes the question, it clearly matters, and matters significantly, to the amateur songwriter.

You may have asked that question.

If you have taken to heart what was said in the last chapter about the song-sharking business, you have no interest in the advertising of "song doctors," "song agents," and various "song services." For example, you understand that to these twilight-zone operators, everything is good, that is, if the fee is paid. They aren't professionals; you want to become a professional.

Therefore, develop a new constructive self-evaluation. Harsh self-criticism should be avoided; it makes for inhibition. A healthy ego, balanced with a knowledge of what you can do, will favor your career in commercial songwriting. It will make you want to excel.

"What Is Good?"

Simply, a song is "good" when it is commercial, meaning that it can be recorded in a studio, and recorded so well that it later will pass a number of evaluations by experts. If the recording does pass these evaluations, effort then will be made to market it. Ultimately in commercial music a good song is one that sells.

An "Iffy" Question

President Franklin D. Roosevelt parried sticky questions at news conferences by saying, "That's iffy."

That is true of the query, "Are my songs any good?" The question can raise issues that are emotion-charged.

Even the pros can become confused if they think too much about intricate considerations of what is good and what is not in song material.

A man whom we will call Harry, an established professional, dreamed of placing a group of his songs in one LP. That is, he had composed a cycle of songs around one theme. He chose to seek out a certain A&R man, or producer, (A&R work will be discussed in detail in a later chapter) who will be called Jack. He wanted a personal interview with Jack; Jack agreed to see him.

Jack listened to the tapes of Harry's compositions, meditated a minute or two, and then said, "I don't think we can do them, Harry."

Harry said, "What's the matter, don't you think my stuff is any good?" Merely raising such a loaded question upset Harry.

The interview ended when Harry expressed a low opinion of Jack's professional judgment. Jack asked him to leave his office.

The Aftermath

Actually the A&R man was not holy; he was human. Too, his company was not the last roundup. "No one has the

"ARE MY SONGS ANY GOOD?"

exclusive on what is good," Dr. Ronald Spores has noted. "Remember those 'hits' that have been passed by and made it further on up the street. Moreover, didn't good old Jack *also* have some doubts as to the *salability* of such a brood?"

As it happened, Jack and Harry had a chance encounter in the parking lot back of the recording company's office building. Tempers were cooled; it was possible for the men to communicate. Harry told Jack he regretted his temper flareup; Jack remarked that maybe he had not made clear what he wanted to say. He went on, "I thought of all our artists and what they do. They don't do material like your group of songs. That has nothing to do with whether it's good or bad material."

An Implication

Some would say that asking for a judgment of your songs in a personal interview is an extremely calculated risk. One A&R man explained, "Many producers much prefer a tape of the material. It's tangible, it can be evaluated impersonally, and, if it's good, it can be passed on to the next person on the line for him to hear. No personalities."

"Are my songs any good?" is a subjective question, however important it is to you. Asking it of friends, spouse, and family members may involve you in difficulties. Friends sometimes hesitate to say what they think. Your best answer will be expressed in the acceptances you receive from reputable publishers for properly submitted compositions.

Ground Rules for Self-Criticism

1. Learn when to give up on a song, temporarily, or forever.
2. Study the form of commercial songs in folios (collections) or sheet music. Write out the lyrics of composers you

like, doing so in the style of writing out poetry in an English class. Note the riming (rhyming), the meter, the structure. Do you know what a couplet is? A refrain? If you learn these technicalities well you are on your way.

3. Danny Davis, creator of The Nashville Brass, urges amateurs to notice that the great composers are masters of brevity.

4. Is your song compatible to your background? You sense that Hank Snow is singing about something he knows in "My Nova Scotia Home." A writer of country music might not be able to write about the sidewalks of New York or a "Chelsea Morning." On the other hand, it's doubtful that a Liverpool composer would attempt the "Ode to Billy Joe" idiom.

5. Is your song a composition? Joe Talbot, a Sesac executive, declares, "Generally, a song should express one central theme or idea in a unique and original manner. Every line should relate to the basic subject matter of the song." Norro Wilson, manager of the Nashville office of the Al Gallico Music Corporation, believes that songs, as compositions, should reflect the standards of excellence of the times in which they are written. Mickey Newbury cautions about the "cancelling effect" of the wrong word or the wrong note. Some pros think that musical compositions should "flow," or have that spontaneity which often is obtained only after much polishing. As in other kinds of writing, unity, emphasis, and coherence are essential goals.

6. Forget the Bob Dylans, Pete Seegers, Woody Guthries, Hank Williamses, Cole Porters, Henry Mancinis, or whoever your idea of a master is. Be yourself. But during your apprenticeship, follow the rules. In time you may break them and establish new ones, but even then, if you are to prosper, you'll be expected to write music that professional musicians can learn readily and play easily for a recording session. Your songs are good when the sidemen can do this and be

"ARE MY SONGS ANY GOOD?"

interested in their content. Rarely is there enough time for learning difficult and obscure material, however technically brilliant it may be.

7. There are many other considerations to the question, "Are my songs any good?" Is the title an engaging one? Some argue that the first word of the first line must catch the attention of the listener. There are others who stress the tag line, or the final line. Ideally, it would seem, a commercial song has both a strong beginning and ending. At present there evidently is a preference for melodic compositions that can be whistled and hummed, but, as we all know, there have been some superhits recently that lacked simplicity of melody.

In evaluating your songs, finally, the avoidance of the personal or subjective element is advisable. Joe Talbot says, "The personality of the performer can unduly affect the listener's opinion of the song. This influence, of course, is not present for a person listening to a recording. Therefore, a live rendition often does not afford an accurate basis upon which to judge a song for recording purposes." To conclude, when you believe your song will pass muster, submit it. If it comes back from X music publisher, try Y publisher just down the street. Y publisher may think it's great. Even after a publisher takes you on, gives a contract, you still may wonder from time to time if your work is any good. That is part of the way it is. Even professional songwriters with many hits to their credit ask the question, and sometimes not so wisely, as we saw earlier. It is best to write another song as quickly as you can and forget subjective questions.

10

Copyrighting and Submitting Songs

Frances Preston at BMI has said that few beginning songwriters have a good understanding of copyright law and its functions. The result can be confusion and misunderstanding between writer and music publisher. The latter normally goes through the red tape of securing copyright, and has the experience and staff to do so. But it is a good idea for you to know about copyright. You can, of course, obtain copyright for yourself. Let's look at both these possibilities, although some publishers insist on securing it.

Copyright in General

Though copyright law needs overhauling, it is the one safeguard for the writer, and for the publisher who gambles on the writer's idea. Seasoned songwriter Cy Coben refers to copyright as "the most unique possession." What it does, basically, is to register a song. If it is an evergreen, a song that lasts, and is listed in catalogues, like "Star Dust," "Blue Skies," or Bob Wills's "San Antonio Rose," it will be recorded hundreds of times over the years and performed countless times in concerts and public appearances. Each time it is recorded, played, and performed you will, under the law, receive a royalty.

COPYRIGHTING AND SUBMITTING SONGS

In general, copyright in the U.S. and Canada conveys nine rights to the owner of a musical composition under the U.S. Copyright Act of 1909:

1. The right to print and reprint
2. The right to publish
3. The right to copy
4. The right to sell or vend
5. The right to arrange
6. The right to adapt
7. The right to publicly perform for profit
8. The right to make any arrangement or setting in any system of notation
9. The right to produce mechanically, as by means of phonograph records, music rolls for player pianos, films, tapes, etc.

Canadian Copyright

Simultaneous copyright of musical composition may be obtained in the U.S. and Canada under treaty between the two countries. After going through the U.S. copyright procedures, as will be explained shortly, write for copyright application: Commissioner of Patents, The Copyright Office, Ottawa, Canada. British, European, and other foreign copyright procedures have been established under the International Copyright Convention. Most North American music publishers look to the Harry Fox office in New York City to secure foreign copyright.

How to Do It in the U.S.

Realize first of all that you cannot copyright a set of lyrics as a song. You can only copyright a *musical composition,* which under the law is an original work "consisting of music alone, or of words and music combined."

Also, sound recordings of your work, such as you might make or have made, are not regarded under the law as copies of your musical composition; they cannot, accordingly, be copyrighted. This is what this signifies: if you submit a tape or a demo record to a publisher, the law as it now stands affords you no protection.

The first step—after you have created a musical composition—is to keep the secret to yourself. Second, by all means write the U.S. Copyright Office, The Library of Congress, Washington, D.C. 20540, and ask for Form E. There is no charge but, as in most dealings with the government, you'll need to be prepared to wait a reasonable time.

Prior to filling out Form E correctly you must write out a copy of your musical composition in some form of legible notation, for this must be deposited with the Copyright Office. If your musical composition includes words or lyrics, they should if possible be written beneath the notes to which they are to be sung.

In the U.S. and Canada copyright is for twenty-eight years; it may be renewed for another twenty-eight years. Get this next, explained Lawton Williams. The Songwriter's Standard Contracts which are used today provide the *publisher* with all renewal rights. This can mean that after the life of the copyright the publisher may renew the copyright. However, if the writer knows about this provision in the contract, he may object and have this provision deleted. On the expiration of the renewal (28 more years), the composition passes into public domain. You probably have seen lists of p. d. tunes; they are readily available. There are instances in which professional songwriters have used a p. d. melody in one of their compositions. "Till the End of Time" uses a Chopin melody, for example.

The National Academy of Recording Arts and Sciences

COPYRIGHTING AND SUBMITTING SONGS

(NARAS), and other professional and trade associations are working to speed along the clearly needed reform of copyright law in the U.S. It should be reported that Congress since 1965 has been grappling with proposed revisions of this law in order to make it relevant to the times and less favorable to inequities for the individual writer. Photocopying and the making of tapes of various kinds obviously drain royalties. It is illegal to make tapes of radio broadcasts, but in scores of thousands of homes it is commonly done without any thought. There are those who argue that the European copyright scheme—for the length of the writer's life plus fifty years—is much fairer than the U.S.-Canadian provision. These matters concern you, so support vigorously the copyright reform movement.

Registering a U.S. Claim

Send the following material to the Copyright Office at the address given above:

1. One complete, true copy of your musical composition. Caution: do not send your only copy. Many writers habitually make corrections at the last moment on the final copy, thinking they will later make corrections on the second copy. Manuscripts cannot be returned by the Copyright Office; the copy you retain in your files, therefore, must be identical to the one you deposit.

2. Application on previously obtained Form E, in duplicate (Form I in Canada). One is returned for your files.

3. Registration fee of $4 in check or money order only. After registration, the Copyright Office issues a certificate to you that your claim has been registered.

Published Musical Compositions

Publication is what happens next. Usually done by a commercial publisher, publishing your songs yourself is precarious. Some 10,000 tiny music publishing firms appeared and disappeared in a recent year in the United States, *Billboard* found.

Publication generally means the sale, placing on sale, or public distribution of copies of the musical composition, as earlier defined. Performance is not publication, nor is limited distribution of professional copies—by the writer—to publishers, band leaders, recording artists, etc. If you are freelancing like this, you may put notice of copyright on these copies to show that your interest in your work is reserved.

The law states that even if your work has been registered for copyright in unpublished form you must produce copies with the copyright notice. Publishers do this, but sometimes composers do it on their own, prior to securing a publisher.

Copyright notice is the word "copyright" or the abbreviation "copr." or the familiar ©. This symbol is essential in securing copyright in countries which are parties to the Universal Copyright Convention. This notice should include the date (year) of publication and the name of the copyright owner(s), and must appear like this: © John Doe, 1970. It must appear on the title or the first page of the musical composition.

If your work is published without the required notice—either by you on an individual basis or by a publisher—copyright is lost and cannot be regained. It's up to you to shepherd your work through all the red tape. The courts have ruled in copyright controversies that carelessness or ignorance is no excuse. Therefore, see to this procedure:

1. Produce copies with copyright notices. Produce the work in copies by printing or other means of reproduction (check to determine how the courts in your area have ruled on photocopies; at present, some courts do not accept them as true "copies," an intricate consideration). Make certain that every copy contains a copyright notice in the correct form and position.

COPYRIGHTING AND SUBMITTING SONGS

2. Publish the work. That is, place copies on sale or publicly distribute them. Many an eminent composer in the past has done this; for example, Beethoven.

3. Promptly after publication send the following to the U.S. Copyright Office: two complete copies of the publication as published with notice of copyright; completed and signed application on Form E; registration fee of $4. Do the same with the Canadian office; follow their instructions.

These three things, of course, can be done by the individual.

How Copyright Concerns You

Through copyright you establish your claim. You are obliged to know that unpublished material needs to be copyrighted, as well as published material.

Experts generally agree that going through the Copyright Offices in the United States and Canada is less subject to possible overthrow of claim than the so-called common law copyright. There is no doubt about ownership, if your claim is genuine. You, as owner, may be in a stronger bargaining position. You may get, say, a third of a penny more in your percentage deal with the publisher, but if your song is a million seller, that extra third of a penny will be impressive.

Contract Writing

Though contract writing at the moment may be remote to your thinking, you would do well to learn how this arrangement works at present.

If you develop into a steady producer of hit songs, you will need a variety of supporting personnel. You may choose a career as a contract writer with a music publisher, in order to have more time for your writing. The firm will attend to copyright details, promote your songs, submit your songs to

SO YOU WANT TO BE IN MUSIC!

relevant A&R producers. You may write for a flat salary, or you may have a percentage deal; but the publisher owns the copyrights of your compositions.

If you continue to turn out commercial material, stir up no personality problems, show business sense, and time your request properly, the publisher may stake you with your own publishing firm as one of his ancillaries. The existing tax structure in the U.S. provides advantages to the publisher under certain conditions. Your little firm may publish chiefly your own songs. Your percentage may be larger. But the big company still retains ownership of the copyright.

You may write under contract for years—these contracts usually are reviewed annually—save and save, and then, like Irving Berlin or Johnny Mercer, strike out on your own with your own publishing business. Who can tell, in all fairness, what may happen? You may compose the next "White Christmas" after you have gone into the business. Then you will revel in the nine rights of copyright, that most unique possession. However, *thousands* of music publishers surface and then submerge every year in the U.S.A. alone. True, you may be able to swing it, but few can; you should know the risks.

Are You Ready to Submit a Song

This is the question for you to confront: knowing what you know now, are you ready to submit a song (you know what a song is now) to a legitimate *publisher?* Your response may be in the affirmative. If so, do you know how to locate a legitimate music publisher? The easiest way is to look through the yellow pages of the telephone directories on file at central offices of telephone companies, but you might get a vanity listing. A better idea is to check with Better Business Bureaus, who have lists of active members that include music publishers.

COPYRIGHTING AND SUBMITTING SONGS

There are 300 music publishers in the eleven-story Brill Building at 1619 Broadway in New York—just one statistic that illustrates how numerous publishers are.

Your assignment at once becomes a matter of refining down your target publisher, and that means you will learn in detail about his current preferences from sheet music and catalogues and folios. You can order these by mail and bone up on them at home.

After having accomplished your first assignment, you are ready to submit your material. As a preliminary, note that it is unethical to submit the same song to more than one publisher at a time. Also preliminary but basic, you understand that hoping for a "co-writer" to "fix" your material is pointless. You are ready when you have gone far beyond hobbying, know that time is valuable, and have the best commercial material you know how to write. You know all the legalities; you have protected yourself. You are ready to take your chances.

Working Outline for Submitting Work

1. Choose your publisher with care. Know what publishers *do*, and know if your material is nearly right for a particular one. "Nearly" is used deliberately, for as Bob McCluskey, a top executive of Acuff-Rose, once stated, "Often even the most spectacularly promising writer has to be brought along carefully over a period of a year or so." In submitting your material, first ask, is it nearly right, say, for Motown? Motown would not be interested in Lawrence Welk-type waltzes without prejudice either way. Apparently Motown has not, as yet anyway, built an audience for waltzes; it *could* happen, but it's not in sight now. Is your song right for Owen Bradley and his Decca complex in Nashville, for Fred Foster and his Monument label? What are they doing? Is your song the sort of material that Ernest Tubb is doing? Or

SO YOU WANT TO BE IN MUSIC!

Loretta Lynn? Diana Ross? Al Martino? Harry Belafonte? Herb Alpert? Johnny Mathis? Or which one of the hundreds of rock bands—in San Francisco, Los Angeles, New York, Liverpool—might do your song(s)? It's challenging to try to command and focus information in vast and specific detail about the music market, but this is what the pros do. As reported, the radio, the recordings on sale, and publishers' catalogues and other publications will be extremely important to your analysis of the marketing possibilities for your songs. So will the trade publications, *Billboard, Cash Box, Music Business, Record World, Variety,* and others, with their charts of hot sellers, their many special editions, and, of extreme importance, their annual directories. These last are international in coverage. They are exciting to read because they show in specific terms, names, places, and sales, how universal recorded sound is. Sound like a lot of reading and study? You're right. A course in rapid reading is seriously recommended to you, such as the ones offered in evening schools almost everywhere in cities of any size in the U.S. and Canada.

2. Having at last chosen your *publisher*—with three or four alternatives if he doesn't nibble at the bait—then *submit* yourself to the agony of selecting from your manuscripts your top two or three musical compositions. That's as many as you should submit (unless everything you write is extraordinarily excellent); too many songs submitted at one time to a publisher by a writer can be as taxing to him as too-long home movies, or too many slides of some friend's year-before-last vacation on Lake Louise are to you.

3. Put these gems on tape: 7½ inches per second. Who does this? You, singing. You're not expected to be Aretha Franklin or Glen Campbell or Floyd Cramer or Chet Atkins. Play your guitar, or piano, or any other instrument that you can play as you sing. At this stage, you're not thinking of Percy Faith- or Henry Mancini-type arrangements, with

COPYRIGHTING AND SUBMITTING SONGS

Arthur Fiedler and the Boston Pops Orchestra as an option, if you can't get either one of them. It's you, singing on tape.

4. You will gladden professional evaluators of your work if you either write out your music or have it done for you. There are professionals who can do this from a tape, but this adds to the bother and the expense. Still, send the music along. The iron rule of selling is: make it easy for the buyer. This doubly and triply and infinitely applies to you at this stage: it is a tough buyer's market.

5. By all means, type out the words of your song, or letter them plainly, and include them with your tape. The final package should be neat, and should include return postage. If you fix your package up in a professional style that will be a small plus factor: be grateful for plus factors in this business to which millions are called, but few thousands are chosen.

6. After having done all this, write a brief, clear letter to the publisher. Find out the right party to send it to (a local disk jockey might be helpful). In the letter tersely summarize your background, give your accurate age (vital if you're a minor, due to legal stipulations), and write as if the Internal Revenue Service will audit what you're declaring. Then state, "I think these songs might be right, with some work, for Marty Robbins, or whoever it is, whatever the market you're attacking). I shall appreciate it if you, or someone, will take a listen, on speculation of course. Thank you."

7. Look again at your package: is it so rigidly put together that opening it may possibly break a secretary's fingernails, even though she uses a letter opener? Mary Lynch Jarvis, Monument executive, often has remarked not unkindly about the difficulties of opening up many a package. A package can be prepared in a way that can tolerate the wonders of the postal service, but yet be opened without trying the limited patience of those human beings who every workday open from 20 to 200 submissions.

8. In due time you will hear from the publisher, usually, but if you don't get the word in three months write or telephone him. As in other businesses, secretaries sometimes enjoy prodding the memory of The Boss. You will get a report in short order.

9. Though it will be troublesome, keep a file box of 4-by-5 cards on which you indicate what you have submitted, to whom, and when. The recurring emphasis on businesslike records may seem obvious, but Frances Preston, head of BMI's Nashville office, advises that all too many songwriters are less than methodical in such matters.

10. Few people like the waiting game. The best way to get around it is to get on with your writing and submitting. Cast your bread upon the waters. You're a kind of salesman, so do as many salesmen do, play the percentages. If you get one out of ten submissions accepted—and this may be far too high—that will be uncommon. Meantime, keep your momentum going and your spirits high. Your mental tone shows itself in any writing attempt.

Totally Optional

Something like this happens often: amateurs hitchhike to recording centers to play their songs for publishers, or to try to get advice from recording firms or established songwriters. Some of these people are extremely persistent and are known as "spooks." They take up a lot of time. They do not realize that it costs a publisher thousands of dollars to bring even the most gifted writer along. Consider what Brad McCuen says, "There are superb writers whose office appearance and personality are negative and they wisely handle business by mail, phone, and very brief office visits. I think this point should be made emphatically to amateurs, who may have seen movies or TV programs or read paperbacks where the personal interview was a living triumph."

COPYRIGHTING AND SUBMITTING SONGS

Along the same line of thought, we might add that it's of dubious value to pitch your songs to artists appearing in your local area in personal appearances. History shows that this is true. The people to "discover" you are the publishers; they are in the business of publishing music. If you have it, they'll want you. Submit, submit, submit, but do so with full awareness of all that's involved.

Finally, even some professionals are unaware of how to protect their material and how to submit it. So, it is not so strange that all too many hopefuls do not even know what a musical composition is. Since they do not know—unlike you—they cherish a hope that some benign publisher will find a co-writer who will fix up their "songs" with music. This has happened, but only rarely.

11

How Songs Are Selected for Recordings

When this handbook was being reviewed in outline form, there were some in the business who responded sharply to the idea of this chapter. These remarks by working recording artists and prospering commercial songwriters may intrigue you as an aspiring amateur:

"Depends on WHO is selecting same."

"Man, are songs really selected, or does it just happen?"

"Wish I could explain how we pick songs for recordings, but don't have time to write a book. It's just a whole lot of work that maybe rests on intuition."

"We live on hit recordings. A song that feels like a hit is all we want."

At least these observations show that selecting songs for recordings is based solely on their sales possibilities. Furthermore, if we know what we're talking about, selecting songs for publication and recording is a highly technical operation that requires many sets of ears, just not one or two sets. It is as nearly objective as any human enterprise can be.

The Chief Aim

The publisher wants material that is commercial. He prints sheet music, and there is a big market for it, bigger than is generally understood. Even bigger, of course, are the fees he gets from the recording firms, which also want commercial songs. Normally, the publisher submits material to the recording firm, though in some cases publishers let long-established writers take their tapes to recording firms—if they are good at it. As a rule, recording firms won't touch unsolicited tapes or demo recordings from amateurs, *for they work only with professionals.* "Working with amateurs gets to be counseling and that sort of thing," one recording firm official explained.

Everybody wants a hit song, but the word "hit" needs to be clarified. In country and western, and rhythm and blues, a hit is 100,000 copies (recordings) sold; a pop hit is 500,000 copies; a rock hit is about 750,000 copies sold. These are approximate. For instance, country and western now sells so well that a minimum total for a true hit is close to 200,000 copies. Super hits are multimillion-copy sellers. The Record Industry Association of America issues a gold recording for a single that sells one million copies and the same to an album with $1 million sales. Only RIAA does this, and only after auditing.

Monies from hits enable companies to buy improved equipment, enlarge staffs, experiment in recording. Very simply, hits make it possible for a given company to continue in business. Some recordings do not move, but for a company to stay in business, the hits must outnumber the misses.

Role of the Artist

The artist who records the song of course is important in the selecting of material, but his role might need to be clarified for you, due to its distortion in some media, notably, certain paperback novels.

Artists are particularly attuned to the judgment of the A&R

man, for he is directly concerned with their careers. An individual artist often plans thoroughly with his A&R man.

In a recent interview Chet Atkins made the extraordinary comment that he may listen to 200 songs before finding one that he can recommend to one of his recording artists. He went on to say that, while he can strongly recommend a song to an artist, he cannot force it on him.

Romanticists may find this last all too dull and unexciting; cynics may be disappointed (surely there must be something else that's being held back, etc.).

In the end, the artist normally acts as the final arbiter of what he will record; if he is an established artist he may insist that the power to decide is in his contract. Artists not yet established generally are required by contract to record what their companies deem suitable to their styles. In either instance, the wise company shys away from demanding that the artist, a sensitive individual, record material to which he clearly does not respond. After all, the artist can project the meaning of the song and give it an impact that will send it soaring to the top of the charts.

Selection of Material (General)

Whatever is recommended, to either the new star or the established star, by the A&R man, or producer, the recommendation is the result of a good deal of discussion and interaction by many persons. In some instances, as with Paul Anka or Peggy Lee, the artist may write his own hit material, which many consider the ideal arrangement in terms of royalties.

The mechanical rights (mechanicals) under copyright are given by a songwriter to a publisher. The latter licenses the reproduction of the composition by mechanical means, including recordings. The publisher gives a mechanical license to a record company, which then pays (to the publisher

HOW SONGS ARE SELECTED FOR RECORDINGS

usually) 2¢ per single recording sold of the given song; the publisher then pays the writer 1¢ per recording, as stated earlier. In most instances, the license fee for a composition included in an LP is the same. At present, the typical recording artist's contract with the recording company (manufacturer) guarantees 2 percent of the suggested retail price for new artists, with up to 5 percent for established artists, based on 90 percent of the recordings sold. Typically, a royalty of 3 percent on 90 percent of the LP's sold is paid the artist.

Obviously, the songwriter who can record his own material, like Johnny Cash, has a better royalty deal. If he is also a music publisher, he is even better off. Many established artists form their own music firms. An example is the late Jim Reeves, whose enterprises now are successfully managed by his widow Mary Reeves.

Remember: any song is selected with an eye to business.

Associated Selectors

You know now that many persons help in selecting songs. In truth, the process of selection starts the moment you drop your package in the mail to the publisher. When it arrives, your song may be listened to by a low-ranking but proficient employee, if the publisher has an open-door policy concerning unsolicited tapes. If the listener hears something that is fresh, he routes it to his supervisor. If the latter is sold on it, he routes it to his superior. Finally, there is a high-level conference. If the song still seems unusual, it will be submitted to a recording company, usually to an A&R man or record producer.

Even after all of this, Harlan Howard says, a star may change his mind about using a song at the last moment—the very moment the producer presses the button that turns on the red light in the recording studio, signifying a recording session is under way. People can change their minds; people do change their minds.

Harlan wanted to show that even established writers and publishers may have material rejected under seemingly weird circumstances. So a philosophical attitude is necessary for the songwriter's peace of mind if he wants to continue to produce. When you do succeed in having a song recorded, you will be justified in marvelling. That means your song has made its way past many barriers, some of them extremely intangible. Even if you could understand all of these obstacles, the knowledge probably wouldn't promote your professionalism.

In simplified form this is what happens to a promising tape or demo recording. It is thoroughly evaluated. If it gets by this, it goes to a deliberately chosen recording firm, where it undergoes another searching evaluation. If all goes well there, then it is recommended to a star, and more conferring, back and forth, results. As one producer summarizes, "We think about how to render it—what musicians to use for the recording we imagine; what studio and engineer for the sound that we also imagine. We also imagine what star can do it."

This is your challenge, then. Write an acceptable commercial song. Be guided by knowing that, if it is good, it will be analyzed as carefully as a diamond is examined by a jeweler. Do try to be philosophical about the "if's." Or as one songwriter said, "I've been lucky in having a lot of stuff published and recorded. I'm glad I don't have to select songs. I just try to write good ones." In short, get on with your writing; it's the only way to attain success.

12

"What's in It for Me?"

For authors, the average income from writing books in the U.S. is reportedly about $1,230 a year. This amount averages all the royalties paid, from mini-sellers to the gargantuan crowd-pleasers like Harold Robbins' novels. Unless they are subsidized, or wealthy, book authors customarily hold 8:00-5:00 jobs, and write when they can at other hours. Obviously, a vast amount of writing is done early in the morning, late at night, and on weekends.

Again there are rough parallels between composing and other writing. Until you have created a string of steadily selling songs, you probably will be working in a nonsongwriting realm. This means long hours and real self-discipline, if you intend to pursue music seriously. Sustaining body, soul, and inspiration will, in all likelihood, and for some years, be rough.

When you become a new professional you will have to haunt the recording studios more regularly than the superstars. You will have to cut endless series of demo records or tapes of your songs. You may be called on to attend recording sessions of stars to advise them on how to phrase your lyrics; you may receive no pay for the time and effort. You will have to keep up your contacts, be reliable, and work long hours when you are not writing.

SO YOU WANT TO BE IN MUSIC!

There are said to be about 35,000 recognized professional songwriters in the U.S. A recognized songwriter belongs to ASCAP, BMI, or the American Federation of Musicians, or other associations, or has a contract with a publisher. These 35,000 possess varying levels of affluence.

As reported, you as a writer get about 1¢ royalty on each recording sold. You get about 5¢ for each copy of sheet music sold. You get royalties from ASCAP, or BMI, or Sesac for performances of your song, or songs, on radio, television, and in various public performances. The basic royalties from a million-copy seller will follow this approximate pattern:

sound recordings	$10,000
sheet music	$ 1,000
radio, TV, etc.	$5,000 to $10,000

If, when all the royalties have slowly trickled in, you have earned $25,000 to $50,000 from your superseller, you are indeed fortunate in the profession. But, as Bobby Lord says, "It's chicken one day and feathers the next." Living expenses will spiral, and royalties may seem so slow in coming, and be all too easily spent in advance.

To live with reasonable stability, you need a steady, tangible income. It doesn't have to be enormous, but it must be steady and assured.

Other Tangibles

As a reminder: songs that appear as the flip side of recordings are as valuable to the pro writer as the once-in-a-lifetime superseller. These are the "catalogue songs" that are recorded and re-recorded. They are steady producers and steady satisfiers to a businesslike writer. Billy Edd Wheeler has stated that his most definite satisfaction results from receiving a royalty check, whether it is for $10 or $100. He added that the stream of checks must flow.

"WHAT'S IN IT FOR ME?"

When you publish a song that becomes a standard, like Doug Kershaw's "Louisiana Man," you can expect a series of other tangibles. The continuing popularity of "Louisiana Man" has buoyed up Doug's career and played a part in getting him on the Ed Sullivan Show and in the Newport Jazz Festival, both of which significantly promoted his career.

How Much

It has been reported that recordings in the New York rock sound can mean a million dollars to their writers and producers. A giant rock seller, under some circumstances, may yield upwards of $200,000 for the writer if he has had a hand in financing an independently produced recording. This is true in Los Angeles, too.

In Nashville, "Music City, U.S.A.," it is reliably said that at least one music publisher recently had under contract a half-dozen composers who were paid $100,000 a year by this publisher. Reportedly, the publisher had a "stable full" of other songwriters who were paid from $25,000 to $50,000 a year.

There are other ways to make money—"the real money," as it has been called. If you can write, make hit records, and take the grind of traveling 100,000 miles a year, and perform well in public, in time you may receive $1,000 and more for a personal appearance. Many touring stars are basically composers (Johnny Cash, Merle Haggard, Bill Anderson). Hollywood's Rod McKuen began as a songwriter, then made it as a recording artist, and now publishes books of his poetry that top the *New York Times* best-seller lists. Rod is the great popular poet of the day. Oklahoma's Roger Miller migrated to Nashville, struck out at first, then made it with "King of the Road." Then he had a brief fling with network television. Now he hits the plush nightclubs, and has a lucrative motel tie-in, thus joining many other songwriters or

SO YOU WANT TO BE IN MUSIC!

recording stars in lending his name and image to a business enterprise.

Intangibles

Intangibles never are to be scoffed at in the pursuit of happiness. Take the proof you can communicate. The continuing acceptance of Bob Ferguson's "Wings of a Dove" —200 separate recordings, over 2,000,000 sales, translation into German, Spanish, Swedish—is satisfying. Its growing number of appearances in church songbooks (fees are not often asked) is pleasing. For "Carroll County Accident" to win the coveted Country Music Association award as "Song of the Year" in 1969 was very good. And for this country song to be picked up by certain folk groups for serious interpretation is pleasant to the composer.

At age thirty—"old" to some teen-agers, or so it is said —Judy Collins, of Colorado, onetime singer of protest folk songs, wrote "Wildflowers," a simple, beautiful exaltation of nature that spun off to a million sales. This was in 1969; it was only the sixth song that Judy had composed. It led to a starring role for her in a Broadway play, and to many other personal appearances, all of which sustained the inspiration of this gracious sensitive singer. Then she cut another million seller in Joni Mitchell's "Both Sides Now."

Judy admitted to the *New York Times* that one of the subtle returns is having knowledge that she can communicate, which is a feat in this age which Marshall McLuhan has described as "fragmented," and the Kerner report called "polarized."

Claude (Curly) Putman, Jr., former Alabama schoolteacher, now Nashville-based composer and music publisher, has more than a score of steady-selling catalogue songs in his bibliography, many hit songs, and, at this writing, one superseller, "Green, Green Grass of Home," recorded successfully

"WHAT'S IN IT FOR ME?"

by Johnny Darrell and Porter Wagoner, and then, with enormous success, by Welsh-born Tom Jones, in London. Tom's reading sold five million copies and led to his soundtrack recordings for James Bond movies, a three-million-dollar deal for a U.S. TV series, and many other tangibles and intangibles grouped under the word "success."

But what of Curly Putman, who wrote "Green, Green Grass"? He says that he wrote it one Sunday morning in his office, which at that time was in Tree, International, on 16th Avenue, South, in Nashville. The idea didn't come as a sudden flash; it had been turning over in his mind for several years. A movie may have suggested some of the idea; song ideas come from everything—things seen, heard, felt, or imagined. When he finally put down the words and music, Curly said he knew it was right. A manly person, Curly said, "You feel like crying when you write something you know is good, you're that happy."

Jerry Reed, brilliant guitarist, singer, and composer, says, "When people ask you to pick and sing your songs, that is something else. But when you know they're accepting you as an artist, that makes the never-ending strain and effort, the splitting headaches, the weariness all worthwhile. Suddenly."

Your Opportunity

The fully prepared professional composer provides poetry and philosophy in times when, allegedly, poetry and philosophy are dead, and are only talked about in university seminars. Popular songs (the identification is not limited to any idiom) play ever bigger roles in religious services, education, educational TV, and other noncommercial areas, in addition to their commercial functions, which also are growing. This thought is offered: the dedicated professional, concerned about the contemporary human condition, has profound opportunities. Look at these words from Charles

SO YOU WANT TO BE IN MUSIC!

van den Borren, president The Belgian Musicological Society: "The sociological connections with which music is involved cannot be over-estimated by any of those, old or young, who wish to learn what it is that governs the nature of music and its various functions in the dynamics of human activity." [1]

Ponder the Belgian musicologist's remark: you are not "slicing bologna" when you write anything. Think of what popular music possibly is to people, so many millions of people. Unless we are badly mistaken, you surely will conclude that your activities—your career—in modern recorded music now offers far-reaching opportunities for tremendous accomplishment. When you really contribute, your earnings and other rewards will reflect your worth to society.

The next six chapters look closely at recording and associated careers. If you are determined and alert in your desire to make a go as a professional songwriter, they will be important to you, in the long run.

---

[1] *New Directions in School Music* (Chicago: American Music Conference, 1969), p. 13.

PART IV
RECORDING AND ASSOCIATED CAREERS

This is the concluding part of the handbook, and it attempts to answer vital questions about the making of recordings, the aura attached by many to major labels and how it contrasts with their real prestige, and other topics that will round out your preliminary knowledge of the recording industry. The economics of recordings are discussed in a way that relates the industry to the overall economy. In this part you are taken into a recording studio for a report on a session by Chet Atkins. You will learn about the producer or A&R man, the sideman, or the backup instrumentalist or singer, what he does, what he is paid, and what he gets out of his work. You will further be given information about the artist, or the recording star. The sixth and final chapter in this part tells about others who help to get the work out.

In reading these final chapters you may realize that there is an internal excitement about the business, perhaps different from what you had imagined, but nevertheless as warm and friendly as the people who work behind the scenes. They are essential, though little known to the countless millions who listen to recorded sound.

13

So You Want to Make a Recording

There are two basic ways to create recordings—either as a producer, or as a recording artist. Let's start with the latter, and see what can happen.

Perhaps you have read the story of how Elvis Presley got started. Even if you have, it bears a brief retelling. If you don't know about how Elvis began, you may be fascinated by the true story.

When Elvis Presley was attending Humes High School in Memphis many years ago, he paid $4 to make his own recording of the old song "My Happiness" in one of those small recording studios that you find in most cities. He did this as a present for his mother, Gladys Presley, whose influence on her son's career was as extraordinary as that of his astute manager, Tom Parker.

Many amateurs not only want to make recordings but do, as either performers or producers, or both. This can only be an "in" thing, but amateurs often make recordings with the thought of entering the business through them. The yen to make recordings can propel you far. Herb Alpert just wanted to make recordings, and used a classic setting to do it—his garage. Now he is part owner (with partner Jerry Moss) of A&M Records and other enterprises. In separate interviews, Connie Smith, Bill Anderson, John D. Loudermilk,

SO YOU WANT TO BE IN MUSIC!

and others, admitted to having "always" wanted to make recordings. A simple explanation is the reality in the background: a successful recording opens up many opportunities. Equally important, in some cases, is the excitement of the recording-studio situation, the way it feels, and the way it is. Pretty Connie Smith has said that she loves the recording studio best of all parts of the music world. She is engrossed with all the procedures that are followed when a recording is made.

You, too, may respond to the unique enterprise of making a recording. That possibly being true, this chapter relates what you need to know and what you have to do if you want to make a recording. Data supplied are generally relevant to recording procedures throughout the world.

Let's now see what happened to young Elvis Presley and his four-dollar recording.

Recording, Radio, Riches

Somehow "My Happiness" was brought to the attention of Sam Phillips, then an announcer on WREC radio, Memphis. Like many DJs, Sam moonlighted. He operated Memphis Recording Studio, which discovered and recorded many songs for a number of major labels. In addition, the energetic Sam operated his own Sun Recording Studio, and in this capacity was the first to record Johnny Cash, Roy Orbison, Jerry Lee Lewis, Carl Perkins, and others, among them, Elvis Presley.

In 1954, Elvis recorded "Blue Moon of Kentucky" and "That's All Right" for the Sun label. The recording sold well in and around the Memphis area; Memphis is located on the Mississippi River in extreme southwest Tennessee, and its trade area includes northern Mississippi and eastern Arkansas, as well as west Tennessee. Some think there is a flavor and a robustness to Memphis that is reflected in the stylings of Elvis Presley.

The success of this initial commercial recording led to a sensational interview of Elvis Presley by Sam Phillips on WREC; it was a smash. There were hundreds of telephone calls to the station afterward; people wanted to know more about Elvis Presley.

The ability of this erstwhile amateur to project his personality led to personal appearances. In 1955, Elvis Presley performed before a convention of country and western disc jockeys in Nashville. The next year, RCA-Victor (now RCA), in the person of the late Steve Sholes, purchased Presley's contract from Sun Records for the then-fabulous sum of $40,000.[1] Since that time, Elvis has made some forty-five recordings for RCA that have sold over one million copies each. A recent million seller was his "In the Ghetto," produced in Memphis by Felton Jarvis.

Elvis Presley now lives in a well-guarded mansion in Memphis. It is reported that he is grossing $5 million or so each year, and could gross more than that, but he does not care to work more than six months a year.

Your Recording

We have no intention of putting down the worthy amateur who chooses to remain in the amateur status. Experience shows again and again that many amateurs are near professionals in their preparation. They render a service to their communities through their music.

Nat Winston, Jr., the nationally known, Nashville-based psychiatrist and hospital corporation president, is an unusual example of the amateur who wants to stay that way. Nat

[1] Jonathan Eisen, ed., *The Age of Rock* (New York: Vintage Books, 1969), pp. 42-56.

SO YOU WANT TO BE IN MUSIC!

has starred for the past several years in traditional folk music festivals in the United States and Canada, picking his traditional Southern Appalachian banjo and singing traditional folk songs. As an outgrowth of this interest Nat has made a half-dozen LPs for Sears in which he, along with Mother Maybelle Carter, tells how to play the traditional banjo, the guitar, and the autoharp. His office states that these LPs for the past five years have had an average total sale of 100,000 copies a year. Nat is an intimate friend of Earl Scruggs, a master of the five-string banjo; Scruggs has written a learned treatise on how to play five-string banjo. But the psychiatrist insisted, in an exclusive interview, that he is happy "just picking and singing," and intends to remain an amateur.

What we're trying to say is this—if you just *want* to make a recording, for whatever the reason, who is to question you? Go ahead and do it; you can learn much from it. And a recording will give you evidence on which to judge your preparation for a professional life in the business.

The basics of making a commercial recording now will be outlined

What You Need

If you plan to survive as a free-lance recording producer you first and foremost need a *money stake*. Your question after this flat statement may well be, "But don't you hear that people make it on just one hit recording that they produce?"

Well, despite his frequent denials of the claim, Berry Gordy, Jr., head of Motown, Detroit-based music complex, often is cited as a man who threw his job away in order to carry out his desire to make recordings. He made a hit recording, and presto! Motown materialized, the story maintains.

SO YOU WANT TO MAKE A RECORDING

The truth is rather different. True, Gordy quit his job on an assembly line in an auto factory ten years ago. But he had previously moonlighted for ten years in the music business in Detroit, getting experience in most branches of the business. He had a money stake, and he had a concept of what he wanted to do, with the writers, engineers, studios, and singers already picked out. He was ready for Diana Ross and the Supremes. Interestingly, one reason for the success of the Detroit Sound, Jon Landau states, is its suitability to the car radio: repetition, very simple, almost a a a a form.[2]

Gordy's career illustrates what has been said already about the fallacies of "dropping out" and the "big break." There may well be instances in which free-lance, or independent, record producers founded a lasting career with just one strong recording, but the Gordy-like pattern appears more nearly the rule.

Inflexibles

It is said often, in writing and on film, that recording music is fantastically flexible and ridiculously inexpensive. It is true, evidently, that Herb Alpert made his first recordings in a garage. So can you, or in a basement, or a rented hotel room. It all depends on your purpose or purposes. If you aspire to market your recording, however, there are inflexibles in the game that you need to know about in advance of your adventuring. Even in so open and individualistic a business as recording, this is true. Whether you desire to perform, or produce, or get your own songs recorded, there are some ground rules that apply.

1. Start with prime song material. Here is the rub if you're a beginning free-lance producer: top material is elusive.

[2] *Ibid.*, pp. 298-307.

SO YOU WANT TO BE IN MUSIC!

You may respond to Donovan's work, which he will appreciate. But Donovan may be reluctant to take a chance on recording with a totally unknown label. How, then, do you procure material? An option, which some have taken with success, is to write it yourself. You're a "double" or "triple threat" if you can both write, sing, and produce recordings, as Bobby Bare sometimes does. Another option is to discover your own writers, which will bring you into direct competition with established publishers.

2. The first step in any journey is the longest. Assuming that you have secured good material, the next step is to attend to all the legalities. You are required, for example, to obtain legal permission from a publisher to record a song held by him. He is to be paid royalties.

3. Renting an adequately equipped sound studio is step three. Electronics and special effects are characteristics of contemporary recordings. Thus the romantic dream of a scratchy, pickup recording, made quickly and cheaply in a hotel room, becoming an instant hit won't hold up. Complex 8-and 16-track studio recorders have made the basement recording almost unmarketable. It may be that a combo can make a recording and lease it to Decca, Columbia, or Capitol, or some major label. But the combo or band must be good; and the electronics must be good. Many acts have started this way, or have attempted to start this way, as Ralph J. Gleason, music writer for the *San Francisco Chronicle* indicates. One band that went "up, up, and away," from just one recording made in a rented studio, is the Jefferson Airplane. According to Gleason, since October, 1965, when the *Chronicle* began covering the performances of the San Francisco rock groups at Longshore Hall, fully 500 of them have made recordings of sorts. Ralph has published the full, incredible list, name by name, in a roll call entitled, "A Roster of San Francisco Bands from Then to Now, the Survivors, the

SO YOU WANT TO MAKE A RECORDING

Immigrants, the Lost." Less than 20 of the 500 have survived.[3] This should make the combo crowd or the country and western band crowd stop and *think*.

4. One recording session can easily cost a minimum of $1,000 cash, in advance of any sales from which the royalties will slowly trickle in. After the recording session is over and paid for, there are other items of expense, as you will see.

5. If you're to free-lance, custom recording is your most practical option. What do you know about custom recording? A custom recording, simply, is one made in a studio, owned and operated by a recording company, or in a facility operated by a company in the business of custom recording. Most recording companies rent their studios and electronic facilities to free-lance producers or artists. Rarely, however, do they pick up the resulting product. Nor can they provide a producer, because the company's A&R men can only work on its own productions, as must be obvious.

Renting a studio for a custom recording is expensive. The rent on a relatively small Nashville studio for a three-hour mono session is about $155; for a stereo session, about $200; for stereo in a large Nashville recording studio, approximately $250. New York and Los Angeles fees are extremely detailed and broken down. The minimum fee for one hour in a New York custom studio is $75 for 4-2-1 track; fees for editing and post-mixing start at $35 for a half-hour. All fees are in ratio to the time of day: 9:00 a.m.-6:00 p.m.; 6:00 p.m.-midnight; midnight-9:00 a.m., with ascending prices to $100 an hour for the studio facilities. Fees for Saturday, Sunday, and holidays are higher.[4]

If you can fund it, or obtain the backing, custom recording

---

[3] *The Jefferson Airplane and the San Francisco Sound* (New York: Ballentine Books, 1969), p. 330.

[4] All figures are based on August 1969 rates.

SO YOU WANT TO BE IN MUSIC!

is one way of getting started, if you are really sure of your material, your performer, and your musicians. The manager of the custom department will help you hire your musicians. What you pay covers the service of the engineer, but not the producer, obviously.

An Essential: Promotion

With over one hundred recordings released every week in the United States alone, there is no escape from the necessity for promoting your product. Here are a few suggestions toward this important end:

1. Send review copies to trade journals. It never hurts to send also well-prepared, brief news copy, along with a top-quality photo (in color, preferably). Remember that many Sunday newspapers in the U.S. and Canada regularly cover recordings; send review copies and news items to them. If your copy is well prepared, it may be run verbatim, thus adding to the potential sales of your recording. Publicity can lead to money in the bank. As for reviews, good notices do not always mean good sales, but they are good for the morale, and they do impress the industry. Keep a file on all your reviews if you can, but remember they concern past work.

2. Send copies to disc jockeys, with a terse personal note. Disc jockeys seem to be ultra mobile and hop from one station to another. You will need to keep up.

3. Telephone calls to DJs help. You may also wish to make a gratis station-break tape for stations. Often they will play your recording after your tape.

4. "Payola" in connection with promoting has received much discussion. Ethical music publishers and recording firms do not tolerate payola, nor does the law. The image of a given company is vital to its remaining in business; a payola charge detracts from a corporate image.

5. Effective promotion takes time, money, imagination, energy, cleverness, aggressiveness, and timing. The total costs for effective promotion will be more than you anticipate. Promotion alone, no matter how competent, cannot make a hit.

Helpers

In this highly technical and specialized business of making a phonograph recording, the solo operator would be lost.

Tom Wolfe's celebrated essay on Phil Spector, "the tycoon of teen," [5] is to the point. Now in his mid-twenties, Spector, an independent producer, has turned out million-copy-selling recordings with regularity since he was seventeen. Wolfe declares that Spector is the wealthiest of the independent producers.

Yet Spector's life is not free and easy. He has no privacy, because of constant interruptions by onetime teen stars, hopeful writers, and last year's rock group craving another chance. The major labels present him with buckshot competition by issuing ten to fifteen r&r (rock & roll) recordings a week, playing the odds. Though allegedly a multimillionaire, Spector lacks the resources and the organization of his competitors.

Therefore, he personally deals with the record distributors. They are his bottleneck, he admitted to writer Wolfe. Some of them will not pay for the records they ordered and then sold, but, as Spector asked, "How can you sue twenty guys in twenty different states?" A distributor may order 1,000 records from Spector the independent. Then when the particular song drops out of the charts, the distributor will buy 1,000 copies from other distributors at a discount. Then he will demand of Spector that he refund the original price and

---

[5] Reprinted in Eisen, *The Age of Rock*, pp. 326-37.

take back the 1,000 records. The refund will be considerably more than the discount Spector gave the distributor. To get on at all, Spector has to go along with this tawdry business.

Spector—as do all independents—subsists on the help of the distributors, and the services, however reluctant, of many other individuals. That he has succeeded testifies to his genius.

The Catch-22 Idea

Joe Heller's novel *Catch-22* probably will be a lasting literary work in its study of the irrational way in which human beings generally perform. In a vague sense, the recording business, to some readers, may seem to function like Milo Mindbender's business in *Catch-22*. Milo Mindbender explains calmly to you, and convinces you, that he buys eggs for seven cents apiece in Malta and resells them for five cents apiece in Pianosa, and *makes a profit*.

Just look what you do with a commercial recording. You take an idea, expressed in a way that's new to the world, and you put it on plastic, or tape. To do this, you, whether producer, performer, or composer, spend money before a cent comes from the product you are making for what you assume will lure a wide market. Is this rational?

There is a real "catch-22," which is the last, final catch that follows all the other conceivable catches. In recordings, you can't spend seven cents, get back five cents, and show a profit. In true business, you only profit when you receive more pennies than you spend on the commodity that you make to sell. That includes what you spend on pushing the product.

14

The "Big Label" Syndrome

The major recording companies at present include Capitol, Columbia, Decca, MCA, MGM, Mercury, the ABC-Dot-Paramount group, RCA, Warner-7 Arts, and a few others. Often, to executives of these big-label companies, come letters that read about like this: "Dear Owen Bradley. OK, I'm ready for Decca to make me a star."

Misguided amateurs often write letters like this hypothetical note to Owen Bradley, or bug A&R men with scores of telephone calls. This faulty approach rests on naive ideas about the business. Almost invariably disappointment and discouragement are the results, plus additional wrong ideas about the business. Many professionals lack the time to try to explain everything that many amateurs want to know about the recording industry and how it works. And a professional quickly learns that he can unintentionally hurt a neophyte's feelings when he attempts to talk about realities.

It is hoped this chapter not only will be useful to the amateur, but, to some extent, will help the industry in its continuing task of educating the public about its principles and procedures.

Are Stars Manufactured?

From time to time you perhaps have read novels that told about a certain big mogul in Hollywood who deliberately fashioned a celebrated star. For example, Lana Turner supposedly was singled out by a very powerful film producer, who happened to see her in a Hollywood drugstore, and was so taken with her that he determined, then and there, to make her famous. Nothing ever is said about screen tests, interviews, or coaching, or the many little parts that preceded stardom for Lana Turner.

When Tin Pan Alley was in vogue, songs may have been ground out, or deliberately manufactured. Hack work exists in any era of man's history, and probably will continue to exist, though Tin Pan Alley is dead and no one has sounded taps. Unless we are completely off course, the strong current now in musical composition is in the direction of quality, as the writings of the composers working in and around Toronto, and the current writings of John Loudermilk, Bobby Russell, and others, prove. Anyone who assumes that quality can be *manufactured* must bear the burden of proving it.

Many people, however, persist in this assumption; they believe that there is a magic wand. A few seasons ago Don Bowman recorded a humorous song entitled, "Chit Akins, Make Me a Star," which was all about a man who thought he was "ready" for RCA and for Chester Atkins' direction. The poor chap couldn't so much as carry a tune, but he was supremely confident that he could emulate Jim Reeves, if only Chet would work his magic. Of course Chet, like Owen Bradley and others who could be mentioned, can bring a talent along to stardom, but first there must be potential.

Slide-rule procedures for picking out hit songs are so scarce as to be invisible. Chet Atkins, a man of rich experience and polished musicality, has said frankly that the only way he can detect a possible hit is to use as a criterion whether he *likes* what he hears.

As has been said, it has to be there; lavish promotion is insufficient. Change the example drastically from recordings to automobiles, specifically the Edsel motorcar. The *New*

THE "BIG LABEL" SYNDROME

Yorker magazine has stated that Ford Motor Corporation spent over a billion dollars in researching and developing the Edsel, an intentionally perfect automobile. Long and detailed surveys of buyer preferences and the subliminal motivation of car buyers were conducted at enormous expense. Every conceivable media of publicity proclaimed the merits of the automobile. But when the Edsel appeared, it failed in the marketplace. If Ford can fail, so can the big labels, the major recording companies.

Misassumptions

It's often assumed by amateurs that the strength of the label will push the merchandise (although a recording all too infrequently is thought of as something other than a product that must be merchandised). That is, that somehow the laws of the marketplace are irrelevant to this business, at least in the thinking of some.

However, as Berry Gordy, Jr. has stated, a producer can give a singer everything, but if the guy can't sing, he won't sell any recordings.

Other misassumptions can get you into tricky issues about *prestige*. In general, the larger the organization, the more prestigious it is. Vance Packard for years has delved into what is prestigious and what isn't. Packard has concluded that prestige is subject to abrupt change when it is a fashion, a fad, or a fancy on the part of the public.

The major labels do afford you prestige, but the prestige that they share with you by recording your songs or your performances, ought to be thought of as a by-product.

What Major Labels Do

You are correct if you assume that the bigger recording companies have the staff at least to secure a hearing for your work.

Moreover, these companies have earned an image of quality and have built up their markets. They share their tradition of success with you, and that gives you status. If you have a contract with one of these well-known companies, it definitely assists you in lining up good bookings as a performer.

The major companies provide many conveniences and services to their writers and artists. They may have a WATS line you can use (and pay for) that will improve communications with the disc jockeys whom you must cultivate. They may have Xerox or other copying machines. There will be many specialists to counsel you; it is their business not only to do so, but to know what to say to you. Major companies pay promptly and pay well. They have competent legal staffs and usually have good contacts with physicians who somewhat specialize in looking after people in the music business.

You also are correct in assuming that it is satisfying in itself to be signed with a major label. This signifies that you have surmounted many hurdles. These companies want only the best; they know how to go after it; they know how to acquire the best.

Finally, the larger companies have the supporting personnel and the national and international organization to promote and distribute your product—your recording. As noted in the last chapter, distribution is the bottleneck for the independent recording producer. He has problems in persuading distributors to take his new label. After this, he may have difficulty in collecting payment. On the other hand, the large companies provide you with the complete merchandising package and have their own field distributors and representatives. In summary, they are thriving corporations, in the business because of their expertise. And the kingpin DJ will always listen to at least a few bars of a major-label product. Even then, there is no surefire guarantee of fame and fortune. If a DJ hears something he likes on a totally ob-

THE "BIG LABEL" SYNDROME

scure label, he will play it and perhaps push it. It is valuable to him to "discover" a new label.

Realities

The biggest of the bigs started as an idea. Just because a label is new, just starting in a modest way, does not automatically rule it out of the scheme of things. This is well known to the already-established companies.

About thirty years ago, Johnny Mercer, Jimmy Van Heusen, and certain others established Capitol Records in Hollywood. Tex Ritter was the first artist they signed. Johnny Mercer wrote the first big hits for Capitol, along with Merle Travis and Peggy Lee. Capitol has contributed to the rise of Los Angeles as the third most productive music center in the United States.

Jimmy Stewart, a native of Middleton, Tennessee, came to Memphis in 1948 when he was only seventeen, in order to work as a runner in a bank. Like Elvis Presley and so many others, Jimmy caught the "bug" of wanting to make recordings. Sam Phillips turned him down, but he formed a partnership with Martin Ellis, a barber, who had some recording equipment. For $200 they made a recording, which, Stewart later said, was "pretty bad."

As time passed, barber Ellis became totally disinterested in making recordings and went back to his barbering. By now, however, Estelle Axton, Jimmy Stewart's sister, had been bitten by the bug; she mortgaged her home to purchase a recorder. Then Jimmy and Estelle rented a vacant movie house; they had a recording studio! In April, 1959, Rufus Thomas and Carla, his daughter, strolled into the studio and announced that they wanted to make a recording. They were in the grips of the bug, too. In May, 1959, Stax Recordings (a name combining the first syllables of Stewart and Axton) released Carla Thomas' "Cause I Love You" in the Memphis

SO YOU WANT TO BE IN MUSIC!

market. Stewart said, "It sold about 15,000 copies locally, and to us that was like having a million seller." At once, Atlantic Records, a big company in New York, sought out Stax, "worked out a deal nationwide, and the record sold about 35,000." [1]

Jimmy Stewart is getting along very well with the company, now called Stax-Volt, and is contributing to the wide popularity of the Memphis Beat (too technical a subject for this handbook, but generally associated with the blues, experts say). You have noted the ten years of effort that preceded "Cause I Love You." Note, too, that Atlantic, like other major labels, had its scouts. There is no indication in Jimmy Stewart's own story that he ever assumed he was mystically ready for the big label to work its wonders for him. When Atlantic did take one of his products, the sales, while respectable, were not sensational. "Cause I Love You" was merely one of Atlantic's successes, mixed in with an occasional superseller. The big label came to Jimmy Stewart and this often happens if a small company can meet the standards of the big time. If you have what they want, they will hear about you, scout you, and, if you measure up, sign you up. Put aside the myths, legends, and romances in order to be stimulated by the fairness and impartiality of the realities.

---

[1] *Delta Review*, June 1969.

15

Economics of Recordings

The recording industry grosses over a billion dollars in retail sales in the United States annually, but as an economic enterprise it survives and grows and squarely depends on pennies and fractions of pennies. How all this works may be rather obscure to the amateur, but it is important to him if he wants to work in recordings. There is a need to provide an overview of the economics of recordings as it relates to larger trends and developments.

Assumptions

In 1958, Harvard economist John Kenneth Galbraith wrote a book with the provocative title *The Affluent Society*. Professor Galbraith called attention in the book to an epochal turn in man's economic life. Throughout most of history, Galbraith argued, the Western nations were poor, but since the end of World War II (1945), most nations have been *affluent*, if only in contrast to their previous standards of living.

The present affluence appears to be a long-range condition. No solid evidence pointing to sudden evaporation of material well-being (in contrast to the early 1930s) is at hand. Along with affluence go inflation, high interest rates, high wages, and high taxes, direct and indirect, federal, state, and local. These assumptions bear strongly on the making and selling of recordings. You may create a recording in an air-conditioned, relatively soundproof studio (they are rarely completely "dead," since dead silence depresses some musicians), but you are not hidden from the real world and its economics.

A further assumption is that recordings are vulnerable to economic ups and downs. At the moment, perhaps, recordings in various forms are status symbols. Experts believe that, to live, man must have music, as well as food, shelter, and clothing. However, if the present affluence were reduced, expenditures on recordings and equipment to play them would sharply diminish. Experts say that a housewife in a financial pinch would no longer buy frozen orange juice, but would return to squeezing the juice from the fruit herself. Even so, though the present boom in recordings is less than twenty years old, it could collapse. For in an era of financial crisis, most people would return to making their own music.

Change

Accelerated change is a constant factor in our technological society, presenting a mixed blessing too complex for discussion here. Understand that *high velocity change* is a constant in the music business.

For example, when a song takes a nose dive in the popularity charts, it loses value instantly. The recording then will be sold at a discount. A recording is as perishable as an orchid. There are few sights as depressing as a stack of old recordings or piles of old tapes. They are junk. They could be melted down and used again, but it is less expensive to start with new physical materials. Old recordings are less valuable than old automobiles.

Few things are as subject to sweeping change—overnight, daily, hourly—as recorded music. If you want proof, just listen to last year's top hit in any idiom. It will sound dated. It is dated.

Expect Higher Costs

Production of commercial recordings is governed by a contract between the industry and the American Federation of Musicians in the United States and Canada. The contract extends to April 1, 1972. Unless the business cycle shows a downward trend, costs of production will go up when the new contract is negotiated.

One recording session of three hours, with ten musicians, represents $1,102 paid in advance of royalties. If the recording is produced on the custom basis, as already discussed, there will be the rental of the studio facilities. If you can record four songs in one session your expenses will easily exceed $2,000. But note this: in most music the trend is for a more elaborate sound, meaning the use of more musicians. If you employ twenty musicians on a session, the estimated total cost figure will increase to $4,000. The times may be changing, as Bob Dylan sings, but the costs of recording are fixed—in one direction: they are on their way up.

Specific Economics

Recordings are portable and therefore appeal to the so-called portable trade; the consumers who buy objects they can carry around. Recordings also appeal to certain car buyers, and to people in industry, business, and education. Recordings are of major importance in the amusement business.

Recordings can be manufactured (pressed) at high speed. American Airlines' Nashville office declared that American in one week in 1968 airlifted 800,000 pounds of recordings out of Nashville for distributions to places far and near.

The sale of recordings to the teen market, which buys most of the "singles," depends on the lure of the novelty or the fad. This accounts for the capriciousness you naturally expect if you write or record teen songs.

In general, young adults and early middle-aged people are the prime buyers of LP's and the more expensive recordings; but teens buy many albums, too.

Whatever your audience—and you'll want as wide an audience as possible—you always confront a buyer's market.

Direct Costs

Direct costs, of course, are those immediately associated with creating a given recording. Musician's pay, arranger's pay, etc. These costs also include promotion, distribution, transportation, press parties, sample copies, long-distance telephone calls, postage, the total spectrum of costs. Take the example of free, or sample, copies. An artist offered this comment: "I would not dream of going to my butcher and asking him for a sample sirloin strip, but I give away a thousand dollars a year in samples of my recordings."

Costs always require a sharp eye and an instinct to detect and eliminate waste and needless expense.

A certain widely respected and eminently well-off artist provides an urn of coffee without charge for musicians on his sessions. This courtesy service controls the distraction of sidemen trooping in and out of the studio during breaks to head for the coffee machines, and their resulting clatter. This artist, like many other pros, maintains "closed sessions" (no visitors) for the same reason—to eliminate distraction. Like any businessman, this artist is preoccupied with production. He is in the studio to make hits; and he has an excellent batting average. The musicians have no objections; they are there to play; the discipline is good.

Indirect Costs

Indirect costs of marketing a recording are numerous. They include such expenses as free entertainment, gifts, non-paid appearances on radio and television, and goodwill gestures. Any artist with a hit record is called upon to give his time to benefit shows. Most artists do so willingly. But it must be realized that these donated engagements, which must be carried off in perfect style, are a drain on the artist's energy. Complete exhaustion, requiring hospitalization with intensive care, is common enough in this business. Guard against accepting too much work, whether paid or free.

In addition, artists often spend thousands of dollars for costumes designed around a hit song, or for elaborate costumes for stage appearances.

All of these indirect costs, and others too numerous to detail, must be borne by your hit recording. You cannot escape them, but then, you probably would not want to do so!

Direct Returns

Your direct returns are your royalties, and royalties have been discussed earlier. However, one fact merits repeating for clarity: give your full effort to establishing a steadiness of royalties. There is just one way to do it: write and work for the long haul.

When your royalties are coming in regularly, practice thrift and habits of savings. Your finances will improve more quickly than you realize.

Other direct returns may include fees for endorsement of products, commercials with a fee and residuals (a kind of latent royalty), television, radio, films, magazine articles, books. If you hit it big and stay big, you'll be approached with offers for an autobiography ghost-written by a journalist. Offers of this kind need careful scrutiny. A bad book will

SO YOU WANT TO BE IN MUSIC!

do nothing for you; ghost-written books rarely have much merit. If you are an effective speaker, you will be asked to speak, sometimes for fees. If you're outstanding, the lecture agencies in Boston or New York may scout you and offer a lucrative contract.

You will be favored with voluminous amounts of "inside information" for making more money, or investing what you have, if you've saved your royalties. Many people will believe that you are richer than Rockefeller. You will need a competent banker and a wise broker to manage your money and permit it to grow.

Indirect Return

You hear it said that people envy those who succeed in doing what they want to do, but most of the time it is the other way around. Many people will be glad for you, and will admire you. Some stars in interviews profess to be disgusted with their loss of privacy, but is this always true? We all like recognition, approval, status. As Judy Collins says, knowing that many people in different walks of life identify with your art is almost miraculous. The joy and happiness that follows an absolutely first-class recording session is unforgettable. It enables you to tolerate the inevitable off-days.

Caution

Do be prudent, but not timid, in your own projections of probable trends in the economy of recordings. Go first-class and be willing to pick up the tab. Be prepared for disappointment. Even the best material will not come off if the human dynamics of the recording studio are awry. Accept the possibility of being "covered," that is, having another artist for another company come along at the same time your recording is released with a recording of a song that will outsell yours. Do as other business men and women do, live with risk, and be energized by it.

You cannot pinpoint the costs of recordings in the same fashion as adding up how much it costs to build a brick wall. Neither can you pinpoint the profits, and the developing sources of profits by normal standards. If you're prepared, recording *is* lucrative.

16

What Happens in a Recording Studio

Very necessary to learning about the recording industry is learning what happens in a recording studio. It has been suggested that you visit a studio—preferably more than one, since no two are alike. Even two studios in the same building will "feel" different.

Studios in New York tend to be small, because of the high rental rates on property. Those in Nashville and Hollywood generally are larger, but in all three cities you will find any number of small, one-room studios. Nashville's studios now produce 52 percent of the recorded sound that is put on the market in the United States, according to Cecil Whaley, public relations director of the Country Music Association.

The "Nashville Sound"

What has caused Nashville's rise to prominence in the recording field is an elusive something called the "Nashville Sound." The term is a convenience used to refer to the effect produced by the total environment and resources of Music City's recording personnel, facilities, and equipment. The Nashville Sound is very difficult to define; different people define it in different ways.

Chet Atkins, one of its prime architects, has described it

as the result of an attitude toward playing that stresses spontaneity. This is saying about music what Wordsworth's dictum says about the nature of poetry, "The spontaneous overflow of powerful emotions recollected in tranquillity." Among the qualities of the Nashville Sound are: improvisations (licks), feeling, power, and simplicity. These are united by the *intense interest* in the final product shared by all the individuals involved in the actual recording.

Though sheet music and formal arrangements are often used, and music stands are common enough in Nashville's recording studios, many sessions do not rely on them. The musicians use simple lead sheets and improvise as they go.

Chet Atkins does not endorse the musicians' unvarying attentiveness to music on music stands, at least for himself and his artists. Once a visiting journalist asked Chet if he could read music. His reply was: "Yes, but I play it by the heart, and not the ear."

Specialists and recording executives come from around the world to see how the Nashville Sound is produced and where it is made.

Recently the president of RCA Mexicana, Senor Cardenas, was Bob Ferguson's guest for a few days. "How," he asked through his interpreter/son, "do you produce the Nashville Sound?"

Having been asked that question repeatedly, and knowing that different people hear the sound differently, Bob replied by asking a question:

"What do you hear in it that is different, distinct?"

Cardenas said that the distinctiveness was in the lack of distortion in the recordings and in the unity of the rhythm instruments: drum, piano, bass, and guitar.

When Ferguson knew what was considered unique in the Nashville Sound, he could then explain:

"We consider rhythm solidarity a basic. We group the rhythm instruments very close together so that they can hear clearly. We instruct all others—lead guitarists, singer, vocal group—to stay with the rhythm. Music is mathematical. Steady rhythm is the mathematical basis—our primary building block. If the rhythm gets 'off' or begins to stagger, we stop the recording, then start another take—often after a practice run for the purpose of seeking the correct tempo for the particular piece being played.

"We are hypercritical of the rhythm—super sensitive to it.

"Likewise, we always strive for lack of distortion—unless we specifically want a distorted sound. At any rate, we want to be in control of it and, for this reason, employ first-rank engineers and maintenance men to make sure we are."

But there is much more to the Nashville Sound. It really reflects the opinions and beliefs of its pioneers and developers as to what constitutes good recorded music. These include Owen Bradley, Chet Atkins, Anita Kerr, Ray Edenton, Floyd Cramer, Buddy Harmon, Junior Huskey, and others.

Just as the name implies, the Nashville Sound is the product of the musical environment which generated it.

Japanese specialists, with their keen interest in technology, came to Nashville to study the physical components of a recording studio. They studied the minute details of tiny pieces of equipment. It is perhaps characteristic of their national interest that they concentrated on technology.

It is perhaps just as characteristic of national interest that the Mexican executive concentrated on rhythm patterns in Nashville's music production.

The "Detroit Sound," like the Nashville Sound, is perhaps similarly deceptive and hard to describe. It is the product of (1) the musical ideas of the instigator(s); (2) the combined ideas of the Detroit pool of musicians; (3) the technology of Detroit recording studios.

Musicians, singers, and recording personnel tend to move to a recording center where they like, or identify with, what is being produced. For this reason, the centers begin to produce a distinctive sound, as San Francisco currently illustrates. To Nashville came those who understood and liked what was being produced there: Boots Randolph, Porter Wagoner, Jerry Carrigan, Connie Smith, Dolly Parton, Tammy Wynette. They had an affinity for the city.

To Los Angeles, New York, Detroit, Memphis, Chicago, and Cincinnati came those who sensed that what they wanted to do was being done in these centers.

This flocking together of "birds of a feather" accounts for the continued emergence of a distinctive "sound."

Where do you instinctively lean in your choice of sounds? Where will you find your flock? By going where you best fit in you can exercise your own creativity. You can contribute to the continuing expansion of an area sound by first being a secure part of its components.

New ideas are deeply rooted in the old. The recording centers are the storage vaults of musical knowledge. Explore these thoroughly, either in person or by listening critically to their products.

"Mr. Guitar"

There are many fascinating personalities in the recording business and Chet Atkins is one of them. He spent his boyhood on a farm in East Tennessee and, though a world traveler, likes to recall his origin, and is loyal to it. He enjoys people from the big cities but has not adopted their ways. He once said, "Sometimes it is challenging to communicate with New Yorkers. When I say, 'Let's get together for dinner,' they think I'm talking about supper, when I'm really talking about lunch. When they say, 'Let's get together for dinner,' I have to stop and think about what they mean."

Chet was given the title "Mr. Guitar" by *Billboard* magazine.

Only he knows how many guitars he has worn out in his

career, but if he is like his close friend Merle Travis, fine guitarist and composer of "Sixteen Tons" and other superhits, a guitar may last six months or so. However, each has favorites that he "makes last"; each is skilled in reconditioning guitars.

Chet's guitars are manufactured to his specifications by the Gretsch Manufacturing Company of Brooklyn. He has long had a close relationship as a guitar designer with the Gretsch people; together they have designed and made "The Nashville," "The Tennessean," and "The Country Gentleman." A Gretsch official writes that these three electric guitars are believed to be the most popular models in the world. According to the American Music Conference, Chet Atkins, in his various roles, has been a chief instigator of the worldwide guitar boom. George Harrison, one of The Beatles, has declared that as a boy in Liverpool he listened incessantly to Chet Atkins' recordings, and was inspired by them to take up the guitar. He plays a Chet Atkins model Gretsch. Chet Atkins realizes that his recordings are studied and analyzed by amateurs and that he must therefore be inventive in his picking (playing). If you become a recording artist, you will discover that your stylings may also be studied and, possibly, copied. To keep ahead of your imitators, you will have to come up with new phrasings, new sounds. Your fans will expect it.

The Studio

The studio where recording is done is a very specialized room. It is planned to accommodate various groups, both instrumental or vocal, providing all the properties needed for the particular effects they may wish to achieve in their music.

A studio has a "personality" of its own. Its individual identity is determined by such things as its size, the properties of the building materials used, the type of acoustical

WHAT HAPPENS IN A RECORDING STUDIO

tiles, and the use of sound baffles. Careful planning precedes construction of a studio, and its degree of "warmth" can be predetermined. In the end, however, only use of a studio will reveal its good and bad points.

Singers, musicians, engineers, and producers are quick to sense the nuances of a new studio. If rhythm players cannot hear one another's instruments, they may be moved closer together. However, if their sounds "leak" into microphones, other than their own, more sound baffles may be placed between the offending instruments. Sound separation—keeping out the leaks—is imperative if the engineer is to have control of the final music mix. Modern microphones, such as the Neuman U-54, allow considerable control.

The final arrangement of the musicians' seating is made at the beginning of, and during, a recording session. Low-volume instruments, such as acoustical guitars, are especially problematic. When mike gain is turned high enough to pick up the sound of the guitar, it often is so high that it picks up surrounding instruments. In these cases, highly directional mikes are a must. The pattern—or pickup area—of such is very narrow.

Studios are constantly modified to improve their qualities of sound. Innovations and experiments are frequent. And new technological developments in acoustics and electronics are incorporated.

Jack Clement's new studio in Nashville was designed with a special enclosed area for the strings (violins, violas, cellos, and string basses) which has a "live feel" that lets the players hear each other better. The result is a better string sound and more security on the part of the string players. It is reasonable to expect that other studios will copy Clement's successful innovations.

To sum up, a studio is not a static thing. Change is constant—even during a recording session—for a studio is the scene of highly creative activity.

SO YOU WANT TO BE IN MUSIC!

Let's Visit a Session

Perhaps a visit to an actual recording session would answer some of the questions you have about this area of the music business. We visited a session in a studio on "Record Row" in Nashville (the district along Sixteenth and Seventeenth Avenues, South, where many of the music publishing companies and recording studios are located) in which Chet Atkins recorded three instrumental numbers with the help of two sidemen.

One of the authors served as the producer for the session. He sat at the control board in the engineer's booth adjacent to the studio where the musicians worked and where the other author sat and observed.

After granting permission for the author—the outsider—to visit the session, Chet remarked politely, "It'll be a lot of work. It may be pretty dull, I expect."

Chet Atkins arrived at the studio for the session promptly at nine o'clock, carrying a guitar case and a kind of attache case as well. He said to a companion, "I was afraid there for a moment I might break a fingernail opening the car door. It's cold. If I broke a fingernail I couldn't pick for a week." He looked mildly horrified at the thought.

He was dressed in a favorite blue blazer, blue shirt, blue cravat, and blue trousers. His ankle-length boots were a well-polished tan leather. He looked pleasant, and retained his soft-spoken pleasantness during the next three hours.

Chet had brought two guitars for a sensible reason: if one broke down, there would be a backup instrument available. He had also brought guitars capable of producing special sounds—either acoustic or electric.

The two sidemen booked for the session arrived at the studio early, as did the engineer and the A&R man. The latter two had the responsibility of checking over and warming up the complicated recording equipment. The two sidemen

WHAT HAPPENS IN A RECORDING STUDIO

were just ready to play. The first, who will be called Henry, played bass; the other, who will be called Jerry, was a drummer. Each of them, though not yet forty years of age, reportedly grosses from $40,000 to $50,000 a year as studio musicians. They are in Nashville's front line of good musicians, and are offered much work in recording sessions.

After greeting the other musicians and technicians, Chet Atkins unhurriedly opened the attache case he carried and leafed idly through the lead sheets it held—perhaps a dozen in number. He finally picked out three sheets and handed them to the waiting Henry and Jerry. His decision could well have meant a thousand dollars in royalties to the composers of the songs he chose.

Henry and Jerry studied the sheets intently and apparently memorized the music at once. Since they are professional, music-reading musicians, they have become masters of the quick study, or rapid assimilation, of music. Their brief study was all the preparation they made for the session ahead of them. They would try to sense, as they played, what Chet wanted in the way of styling or treatment of the songs.

With no discernible flurry or abruptness, Chet and his sidemen were trying out the first of the three songs within seven minutes after he arrived. During the next three hours, Chet Atkins managed to record less than nine minutes of music, instrumental readings of "Drive-In," "Mercy, Mercy, Mercy," and "Autumn Leaves." The compositions demonstrate Atkins' well-known versatility: one is a jazzy work, one is contemporary rhythm and blues (meaning that it is influenced by rock and by country), and the other, "Autumn Leaves," is an evergreen, almost a pop classic. And each one of the compositions is difficult music.

The working style of the guitarist came to rival our interest in the music that he was interpreting, with his well-recognized purity of notes, steady rhythm, and unexpected variations and improvisations that in no way detract from the melody. Chet appeared to be striving for relaxation and concentration, sometimes hunching over his guitar until his chin nearly touched the strings. Sometimes you could hear him sigh. He would stop a moment, take a quick puff from a stubby cigar, and then launch anew what seemed to be a fascinating contest between his guitar and his will to make the instrument say what he wanted to say.

Seven "takes" were needed on "Autumn Leaves." (A take is each attempt to record a composition.) Some takes are merely false starts, others are long false starts, and yet others are a full playing of the song. During rehearsal, tape machines are not rolling. When performance is satisfactory, tape machines are started, the engineer calls, "take one," and the actual recording is begun. The assistant engineer, or technician, keeps a record of the takes. There may be many starts and stops before the artist and producer are satisfied.

After take five, Chet observed, to no one in particular, "Well, I think I played that pretty well for a hillbilly."

"Want to hear it, Chet?" the producer called over the intercom connecting the studio and the engineer's booth. Still amused by his hillbilly remark, Chet grinned and answered, "No, let's try another one."

The three songs appeared in the LP *Solo Flights,* which has been both critically and commercially successful, thus proving Atkins' consistent contention that, if you are a professional, you can please both the critics and the consumers. *Solo Flights* contains commercial but interesting music and contained at the time it was made, a number of innovations. Since its release Chet Atkins has gone on to other things, such as recording again with Arthur Fiedler and the Boston Pops Orchestra, again showing his belief that a professional must seek out new approaches in music.

The recording session that is being discussed gave an opportunity for Chet Atkins and his sidemen to bring into focus their professional preparation. It would be wrong to assume that the session typified recording sessions everywhere, or that it was uniquely superb. It was a highly effective session, but the demands and rewards of professional dedication are hardly limited to Nashville, or New York, or San Francisco, or Detroit. When you give to the recording situation wherever its geographical location, you are a professional. Once again, secure permission to visit a recording studio to see and feel what it's all about!

The Other Side of the Coin

A recording session can be just the opposite from the one described here. A session can develop into a headache on the part of all, a trying ordeal. The product that is produced under such unfortunate conditions as will be briefly describe will be so flawed that thereafter it will be "kept in the can." This is an inelegant but graphic phrase for what happens to the taping of a bad session that the company, or companies, dare not release because the quality is so poor.

Here then are some illustrations of bad sessions.

Let us say that you are a songwriter and you have a contract as a recording artist. The recording company may ask you to record the compositions of other writers. If you have had some personal difficulty with writer X in the past, or you do not like his work, you may not do your best in singing his songs in the studio. The material may seem empty to you, wordy, corny, dull. You may complain, strenuously, to the A&R man, to the sidemen, or to yourself. Or, in another instance, an artist may be late for a session and cause the musicians to wait for half an hour. The musicians will be cold, not ready to play. Some will be upset, some will be irritated. Other times, an artist may not know the material, which can cause problems and delays. The musicians have come to the studio to pick, not just to sit and wait.

Those artists who survive and grow, like Porter Wagoner,

SO YOU WANT TO BE IN MUSIC!

prepare themselves in depth for every possible contingency before a session. Porter and his staff confer creatively with the record producer and reach a definite decision about the compositions to be recorded. The musicians to be used are decided upon (they always include Porter's own band, the Wagonmasters). The design of the LP jacket is planned; the writer for the liner notes is selected. Nothing is hit-or-miss about a Porter Wagoner album. Stars like him are in the business of making hits. Working in a meticulously planned recording session is a privilege, indeed.

Summary

What happens in a recording studio? It's interplay and interaction of many personalities and many skills, a kind of meshing process. It's a test of all persons involved, for in recording musical sound you continuously must prove and re-prove yourself. If you're willing to contribute and are fully prepared, there's a place for you in the studio.

17

Studio Sidemen

A sideman is a man or woman who plays a musical instrument as part of the accompaniment for the star of a recording session. Sidemen may also be vocalists, like the Jordanaires. The Jordanaires first became stars in their own right on Elvis Presley recordings, particularly for their "do, wah, do, wah" vocalizings for Elvis. The Jordanaires now have all the work they care to do.

The one you see backing up the star on stage, television, and in films is also a sideman. The term connotes anyone who acts in a supporting musical role for the featured performer.

The proficient sideman is far from an incidental personality: he contributes to the sparkle of a well-executed recording session. Observation shows that he often comes up with the right lick, or improvisation, at the right time, for the artist when the latter somehow isn't quite developing the material. So a sideman is appreciated and valued, is paid accordingly, and enjoys the privacy denied a star. If he consistently proves himself, the good sideman has more offers of work than he can take.

Earnings

These instrumentalists or vocalists whose names are unknown to the consumers can hit it big. The manager of one

SO YOU WANT TO BE IN MUSIC!

recording company in Nashville recently told Dudley Saunders of the *Louisville Times* that between twelve and fifteen of the musicians who work his studio earn from $25,000 to $40,000 a year "laying down backgrounds" for the stars. Others think these figures are middle-of-the-road. The average studio musician probably earns a minimum of $15,000 a year in Nashville, with the top echelon receiving up to $50,000 a year and more. There are known to be a few top-flight sidemen, who can work well in the New York, Nashville, and Hollywood centers, who hit $100,000 a year. Common requirements are skill and a willingness to work long hours.

Perhaps Irreplaceable

Under the present dispensation, the accomplished studio musician may well be nearly indispensable. If he is highly accomplished, he enjoys a better chance for longevity than the star, with infinitely less bother. As one sideman observed, "You're able to give all your thinking to music."

RCA and Westinghouse have manufactured music synthesizing machines that produce music-like sounds virtually by push buttons. The electronic age is upon us, and amplification is no longer achieved only by mechanical means; any musical instrument per se is a mechanical means for amplifying but tubes and transistors and things like that are now involved. What you do is set up an electronic wave and then modify it, or synthesize it.

The Moog (pronounced Moag) synthesizer has been developed by Robert Moog in his studio in Trumansburg, New York. In theory, his synthesizer can reproduce any sound in nature, from violins, drums, trumpets, birds, running water. It can also combine these sounds so as to produce totally new sounds.

STUDIO SIDEMEN

RCA producer Andy Wiswell in New York for some time has been fascinated by the potential of electronic music, which he contends is no more "synthetic" than piano music. Sid Bass has created arrangements for one of Andy's recording adventures with the Moog synthesizer, using eight-track stereo equipment. First, the tracks of the "rhythm section" (six instruments) were laid down and the passages for two tenor and two bass trombones that Sid had written. Then Andy and Sid took the tape to Trumansburg, New York, where Bob Moog set up the equipment and programmed the synthesizer to produce the sounds. The result was a successful LP entitled *Moog Espana,* arranged and conducted by Sid Bass, and of which it has been said: "The result is unique. This is a glimpse into the future—a glimpse in the direction in which much of music, popular and classical alike, may be going."

The LP includes "Granada," "Mama Inez," "Malagueña," "Spanish Flea," "Lady of Spain," "Valencia," "The Peanut Vendor," and others that remind you of the rich and honorable place of Spanish and Spanish-like music in the world, another suggestion of the *internationality* of music. And the impact of the sound is roughly the equivalent of other recorded sound: it is electronic.

If, perchance, any sidemen, arrangers, or conductors happen to read this discussion of the Moog synthesizer and are horrified at the prospect of being replaced, the reaction is understandable. To apply a platitude, electronics is bigger than any of us. It is better to be informed than to not know what is going on; but the player piano never superseded the human-played piano; recorded sound never displaced live sound. There are more amateur musicians now than at any time in history, and there are more people, too. In the world of recorded music, the sideman is necessary. Automated music, of one kind or another, has waxed and waned.

SO YOU WANT TO BE IN MUSIC!

An Informal Portrait

This is an informal sketch of a recording studio sideman, who will be called Randy, and who regularly worked the three major recording centers in the United States. He is in his forties, and has been in music one way or another since boyhood. Once he successfully recorded as an artist, but now says, "I tired of the star bit, three weeks on the road, three days at home." Randy sports the so-called studio pallor that identifies men and women who spend eight to twelve hours a day in studios. He may work three sessions of three hours each, seven days a week, in seven or more studios. He may even work four sessions a day, or even five. Like many sidemen, Randy drives a late-model, gleaming Cadillac and dresses with a quiet elegance that doesn't come off the pipe racks.

Like other sidemen, he brings his lunch and dinner to work. Some sidemen prefer lunch kits, but Randy uses an attache case for his sandwiches. Again like others, he has been observed taking a spoonful of honey for quick energy during a session that was having trouble getting off the ground. He smokes cigars, but limits himself to six a day.

In conversing with Randy you notice that he is soft-spoken but gives off an air of formidable personal security and self-confidence. This, too, is characteristic of other greatly accomplished sidemen; they know they're good. That Randy enjoys reading is evident when you talk with him. Though he argues that novels are a waste of time, preferring solid fare like history and biography, "anything factual," he is quick to add, "Every guy to his own bag." With the aura, in other words, goes a high degree of tact and social skill.

Yet Randy can offer his opinions in a way that avoids friction. He ardently dislikes losers, phonies, hangers-on, and lacks a high opinion of journalists. He is disciplined about his time and energy, and can dismiss you with the ease of a busy clergyman.

Randy has been observed in action, at least once, in a session with a star who was in the throes of a temperamental upset. Randy reacted to the star by attending strictly to his part of the assignment, thus suggesting his self-discipline. He excels in the art of making a suggestion, waiting his turn. That is, he will hum, sing, or whistle a transition in the music, which has been throwing the other sidemen. Often, his improvisation is acceptable to the artist, producer, and the other musicians. Since Randy so evidently contributes, he is in high demand.

Randy says, "I like my life. I make a good living. I'm doing what I want to do."

In summary, Randy is a specialist. Except for "utility men," who can play a variety of instruments (usually referred to as "doubling"), all studio musicians are specialists. A utility man can play rhythm guitar, or lead guitar, piano, or bass. He, too, is valued and paid well.

Pay and Working Conditions

Because of a musician's intimate and lasting relationship with the Musician's Union (American Federation of Musicians), a detailed study of present union regulations is of value. The AFM includes both the United States and Canada. Under the contract between the union and the industry that continues through April 1, 1972, these are the regulations for recordings, jingles, and video tape:

1. A session is 3 hours, 4 sides (songs) maximum, and total length of music recorded is not to exceed 15 minutes. Including health and welfare, the pay is: $86 per sideman; $171 for leaders and contractors. (For information on these last see the next chapter.)

2. Overtime allowed is one half hour, during which one

SO YOU WANT TO BE IN MUSIC!

side may be recorded: $23.40 per sideman; double for leader.

3. Premium time is after midnight (except the 10 to 1 sessions), and anytime on Saturday, Sunday, and holidays.

4. Premium session pay, 3 hours: $121.40 per sideman; $241.20 for leader.

5. Overtime allowed is one half hour, during which one side may be recorded: $35.10 per sideman; double for leader.

6. The Federation is responsible for negotiations in regard to synthesizers.

7. Pension payments: 8%.

8. Once called, a session shall not be cancelled or postponed less than 7 days prior to the scheduled date. In an emergency, a session may be cancelled or postponed only with the consent of the office of the president of the local musician's union.

9. Two rest periods of 10 minutes each, after the start of the session and before the ending, are to be provided.

Other Provisions

Cartage (payment to a musician for transport of his instruments) is: harps, $14; drums, bass, tuba, baritone sax, cello, and all amps, $3 each.

Instruments are divided into two categories, as follows:

Category I, fretted instruments, includes 6-string rhythm guitar, 6-string electric guitar, "combo" guitar (rhythm and electric guitar combined), 6-string (steel), round-hole guitar, 6-string (nylon) classic guitar, 12-string acoustic guitar, and 12-string electric guitar. The contract states that playing two of these instruments is "no double," but for each additional instrument in the category "it is a double." The pay for the first double, based on a three-hour session, above the regular pay given, is $14.04. Each additional double is $10.53

STUDIO SIDEMEN

above the normal pay. Flute and piccolo, oboe and French horn now are doubles.

Category II includes all other fretted instruments, such as dobros, ukeleles, and banjoes. Along with any of these stipulated instruments, if you also play an electric bass, it is a double. If you play instruments from both Category I and Category II, this is a double, at the pay reported.

Use of electronic devices such as multiplex, maestro, multiplier of octaves, etc., to be treated as a double, at stated pay, if used to simulate instrumental sounds in addition to normal sounds of instruments to which they are attached.

If the company requests musicians to bring a doubling instrument and the instrument is not used, the company must pay the musician $3 anyway. If any musician overdubs during a session, full scale must be paid to the individual.

Who keeps up with the charges? The musicians fill out forms after a session that go to the company, which has people who check these forms for accuracy. Many musicians keep their own records. In general, the union arbitrates questions about pay, but the session leader keeps up with the charges. This explains his pay.

October, 1970

Effective October 1, 1970, sideman scale, including health and welfare is: $91 per formal-time 3-hour session; $181 leader. One half-hour overtime pay is: $25.07 per sideman, double for leader. Premium-time (previously defined), 3-hour session, $128.60 per sideman, double for leader. One half-hour overtime: $37.60 per sideman, double for leader.

National Jingle Rates

A national jingle is one used outside the jurisdiction of a particular union in whose jurisdiction it was made. One hour session, maximum of 3 jingles, for the same company: 1 musician, $81; 2 and including 4 musicians, $44.30; 5 or more musicians, $41. Leader and contractor (if any) are paid double the pay for 1 musician. If a jingle is used on both radio and TV, the above rates are doubled. The above rates include the $1 health and welfare contribution.

Overtime: 1 through 4 musicians, each 20 minutes, $14.43; 5 or more, $13.33; leader, double.

Doubling: 30 percent of scale for first double; 15 percent for each additional double.

All the above are subject to pension payments. Cartage is identical to commercial recordings (see above). This likewise is true of overdubbing during a session, and of the use of electronic devices, as previously defined and described.

Reuse payments are as follows. A jingle may be broadcast for a period of 13 weeks from the date of the first broadcast. If used beyond the 13 weeks, 50 percent of scale must be paid to each musician for each 13-week cycle. Five percent of scale must be paid into the pension fund.

Local jingle rates, at present, are the same. They can be broadcast for one year from date of first broadcast: sideman, $36.00; leader, double; plus 5 percent pension.

Network and Video Tape Syndicated Shows

For a half-hour show, including four hours' rehearsal on the same day, scale per man is: $60.94.

For an hour show, including four hours' rehearsal on the same day: $97.68.

Leader: double the above rates.

Rehearsal pay, per sideman: one hour, $13.40; additional time of each fifteen minutes or fraction, thereof, per man: $3.35. Leader is double.

Doubling: 25 percent of the basic scale extra for the first doubling, and 10 percent extra for each additional double.

Time allowed for the above scales must be within an eight-hour span, excluding one-hour meal time. Any time beyond the eight-hour span is paid time and a half.

Syndicated shows may be broadcast on any number of stations one time. If broadcast more than once, 75 percent of scale must be paid each musician, plus the 5 percent pension.

How You Can Become a Sideman

If you are confident that you can *contribute* to a recording session (contribute, as has been described and defined in this handbook), one possible choice is to seek work as a sideman for demo records in recording studios in your hometown or a nearby community. There are hundreds of smaller companies in the United States making demonstration records for submission to larger companies. You will be paid about $10 a song or less, and you will "work for hire," meaning no royalties. After seasoning yourself, write to an A&R man whose work you know and like, and say something like this: "I have been working demo sessions for a year or so, belong to the union, and would appreciate a chance to try out on one of your sessions." List two or three of his artists, with a terse comment about their most recent recordings.

It may well be that the producer (A&R man) has heard some of your "backgrounding." Your letter may jog his memory. If you are good, he'll do his best to use you.

It Can Happen to You

For the first time, the documented story of Boots Randolph, widely admired for his saxophone innovations, can be told. Thanks to Spider Rich, a perceptive and talented music man, who operates out of Henderson, Kentucky, just across

SO YOU WANT TO BE IN MUSIC!

the Ohio River from Evansville, Indiana. Since the Boots Randolph story is becoming subject to myth, we are delighted to present Spider's authoritative account.

I first saw Boots on a local TV show. Then went to hear him at a nightclub in Evansville, Ind.
    I enjoyed his playing very much and realized what a great talent he was.
    I asked him about recording. He was very nice, but wasn't interested.
    I invited him to my home. While he was there, I recorded some instrumentals on tape that I was sending to Chet (Atkins). By the way, the instrumentals were "Siesta" and "Backwoods" which later Chet recorded. But so Chet wouldn't miss Boots's playing, I put it on the first part of the tape.
    I was in Chet's office a week or so later. He asked me if I knew the sax player on the tape. I said I sure did, that's why I had him on these. I wanted Chet to hear him.
    Chet said, "We could use him. Can you get him down here?" I said I'd try. I told Boots, and he wouldn't believe it. They had a session the day we went down and Chet asked the guys (sidemen) to stay afterwards, and he called Owen Bradley to come over.
    Boots played "Bill Bailey" and no one could believe what they heard.
    From then on things started happening for Boots.
    And I must say it couldn't have happened to a nicer guy or a more deserving one.

Yes, it can happen like this for you, but be prepared, as Frances Preston suggests, "for the suddenness, the flood, of other opportunities after you really break in." Frances added that every aspect of your personal life will be affected —how you walk, talk, dress, eat—even how you think about yourself. All at once you will be expected to meet and maintain the highest standards of the profession.
    Remember, music publishers and recording companies are always looking for superior talent.

18

Others Who Get the Work Out

A salable commercial recording results from the coordinated efforts of a wide variety of skills. The recording session is but a fraction of the total man-hours invested in the prelude and the postlude of the initial recording. This final chapter, in effect, rephrases in sharply specific terms the concept that recording is an organized business that offers career opportunities now, with additional opportunities emerging rapidly.

Accountants

It is of supreme importance for recording artists, sidemen, publishers, recording companies, and associated or supporting businesses, to keep accurate books. Royalty statements, for instance, must be read and understand by all parties, especially composers. Tax problems can be particularly messy in this business. If you are trained in accounting, you may free-lance for a few seasons and build your practice in music circles. Another avenue you may follow is to apply for work as an accountant with a publisher, a recording company, or an artist or writer. The main offices, in New

SO YOU WANT TO BE IN MUSIC!

York, of ASCAP, BMI, SESAC, Harry Fox, and related businesses require accountants and auditors. College graduates with majors in accounting may also investigate job opportunities with accounting firms that have music as a specialty. Starting salaries for college-trained, beginning accountants in general accounting firms are about $7,500 a year, according to the U.S. Department of Labor. The top pay for certified public accountants (who have passed the examination of a state board of accounting) exceeds $100,000 a year, according to the American Institute of Certified Public Accountants.

Advance Men

These individuals spearhead personal appearances by stars or by "package shows" (groups of stars). There is no way of determining what their pay is, but some of them are known to live comfortably. An advance man is skilled in obtaining publicity in the news media. Obviously he travels a lot. He works under pressure and must be expert in negotiating, bargaining, and in reading contracts. Every big act requires advance men. In some instances, advance men entered the field after working in journalism or advertising.

Agents (managers or bookers)

Probably the best-known talent manager is Tom Parker, who has guided Elvis Presley's career for many years. Before Elvis, Parker had managed Hank Snow—and before that time, he had managed Eddy Arnold. Top agents like Parker handle only one or two stars. Other agents, generally termed bookers, handle a fairly long list of active clients. The booker secures, and handles the contracts for, show dates for the artists. He is often not as intimately associated with the

OTHERS WHO GET THE WORK OUT

artist as is the personal manager. You enter this line of work only after considerable experience in many aspects of the business. To become a Hubert Long or a "Lucky" Moeller, your contacts must eventually be worldwide, and your business sense must be acute. If you can work well with many kinds of people, and put in long hours, you eventually can earn big money. One way to start is to apply for a job with an established talent agency, a top booker, or successful manager. "Work your way up" appears to be the rule for making it in this interesting profession.

A&R Men (producers)

The basic task of the producer is "matching" the artist with the proper song material. The latter comes to the producer from the music publisher.

A conspicuous example of an A&R man is Jimmy Bowen, in his early thirties, who produced such giant hits as "Strangers in the Night" and "That's Life," both by Sinatra, "Everybody Loves Somebody," by Dean Martin, and also created big-selling LP's by Bing Crosby and Sammy Davis, Jr. Outside the trade Jimmy Bowen's name may not be recognized, but his company, Amos Productions of Hollywood, sold over 2,500,000 single recordings and 850,000 albums in 1969. The A&R assignment provides challenge and opportunity. You may want to know how to become an A&R man, so here are some pointers.

The A&R man is the record company's most direct agent of contact with its recording artists. He is also known as the record producer, or simply producer. As his title implies (artist & repertoire director), he is responsible to the company for the artists under his direction and for the music they record (the repertoire). His task is to select hit songs from the immense number that reach him through the mail and direct contact. It is also his task to match the song, singer, studio, and musicians. He also must generate ideas for albums for his artists, and he must come up with new ideas for singles—and, in many cases, persuade the artist and the company to go along with his ideas. For this he needs both tact, and the respect of others. He must also generate excitement in the studio, elicit the desired response from the musicians and engineers. In the eyes of the company, the A&R man alone is responsible for the final product of his artists. In the eyes of the artist, his A&R man is his guide, advisor, and companion, as well as his most direct contact with the company he records for. It is to him that the artist directs questions, comments, complaints, and ideas. It is with him that the artist plans his career in the realm of recording.

The A&R man, like the artist, musician, or songwriter, must prove that he "has what it takes." Like the other creative members of the team, he stands or falls on the material he produces. They say that an artist is "as strong as his last record." The same is true of the A&R man. He must produce successfully—that is, he must produce salable material.

Where does an A&R man come from? He may come from the ranks of great musicians who prove to have a knack for producing. That is where Chet Atkins came from. He may come from the ranks of the observers who attend recording sessions whenever possible and have a burning desire—and a belief in their ability—to produce records. That is where Felton Jarvis came from.

They may also come from the field of big bands, where they were bandleaders, or lead vocalists, or musicians. That is where Danny Davis and Owen Bradley came from. They may be intimately associated with another facet of the music industry—perhaps as a DJ or promoter. Or they may simply enter the music business for the sole purpose of becoming a producer.

From whatever source they come, they share in common the desire to produce. They must believe that they can produce as well or better than anyone else. With this belief they must couple the experience of handling the studio situation. They must get along with people under highly charged conditions. Studio experience can be gained in the many ways already mentioned—as a musician, engineer, arranger, etc.

One of the best producers today, Jim Malloy, entered the A&R field only after years of experience as an engineer. As an engineer, he was one of the best. Singers and producers flew great distances to use his services. Jim had ideas; he injected them into his work. Now he is well on the way to becoming a top producer as well. Like many top producers, his problem is to keep his roster of artists small enough to give each artist the personal attention he deserves. He is now in demand as a producer.

Jim's example serves to point up the need for a close knowledge of what happens in the studio situation. Jim gained it firsthand as an engineer, merely transposing it to his new role as producer. He had the desire to produce and he had the "know-how."

The apprenticeship role is important for the would-be producer.

The income of the producer is directly dependent upon his ability. He can start with a salary of $10,000 or $15,000 per year, depending upon his reputation as an "independent producer," but his income is supplemented by bonus or "incentive pay" which is almost unlimited! As with the performer, his income depends upon his acumen.

There are many successful independent producers. They are called upon from time to time to produce records for various companies. They rely upon the sales of the records they produce for their income. Many of the independent producers handle certain artists all the time for a given company. This is because the artist works well with the producer and it is advantageous for the company to keep the relationship intact.

While the road to becoming a producer may be round about and hard to define, we can point out three essential ingredients:
1. The desire to produce;
2. Persistence in mastering the essentials of the studio situation;
3. The basic ability to get along with people—to work in unison or harmony.

Arrangers

Bill Williams, southeastern editor of *Billboard,* has pointed out that arrangers now are in demand in nearly every musical idiom. An example is Bill Walker, an Australian who migrated to Nashville via South Africa to do the orchestral arrangements for Eddy Arnold's recordings, and for others. Ray Price's superhit for Columbia was Cam Mullins' arrangement of "Danny Boy." Cam sometimes directs Ray's orchestra in concert appearances. Atlanta's Don Tweedy arranged Bobby Goldsboro's United Artists giant "Honey." Bill McElhiney's arrangements for Brenda Lee, starting with the million-sellers "I'm Sorry" and "All Alone," have made him rich. Anita Kerr, once a Nashville arranger, has transferred to Hollywood; Rod McKuen uses her arrangements. You'll need a thorough musical background in this field. One way to get started is to work up arrangements for local bands or combos. When you have acquired knowledge of instrumentation, harmony, and rhythm, and, in your judgment, possess a certain flair, select an A&R man whose work you know and like and write to him. Ask for permission to submit an arrangement for one of his artists. As was stated earlier in connection with songwriting, you are obliged to know what is being recorded, by whom it is being recorded, and who produces it. Study and research are obvious requirements.

Contractors

This field is open to women as well as men. Traits of tact, diplomacy, and mastery of detail are important, for your job, essentially, is to "hire the musicians." In practice, hiring musicians requires skills in persuasion, for the really good musicians are in demand and may pick and choose their jobs. Skill with the telephone is also important. The role often develops as a lucrative sideline to some other job in the business, for you need to know many people, and know them well. You can earn as much as you have time to work: sideline contractors in Hollywood are said to pick up $10,000 a year, or more, in their moonlighting. Contracting is highly creative work, or, as one contractor said, "You do your part to get all the musicians together at the right time and at the right place." There are relatively few full-time contractors at the present time. One beginning approach is via a clerical job with a recording company. Some recommend the smaller though well-established recording firms, "because you get to do everything."

Engineers

Acoustical engineers, assistant engineers, and technicians are found in the control room—before, during, and after recording sessions. If you have visited some studios, you have seen them. They do much more than work the "push-pull circuit" with its scores of knobs and levers. They have the knack for producing recorded sound; every engineer's sound, believe it or not, differs from other engineers. Before the session they check out the complicated equipment as carefully as the pilot checks out the controls of a 727. During the session the engineer is expected to grasp and respond to the effect the producer and the artist are striving for in a given song. After the session the engineer works with the producer in editing, blending, mixing, and overdubbing, operations requiring many more hours than the session itself. Engineers also work sessions in which harmony or additional instrumentation or effects are added to the master tape. Typical avenues of entry into this vocation are radio and television sound engineering, but Cal Everhart, who is well versed in most areas of the business but now specializes in studio management, advises that home study courses are available for anyone wishing a first-class radio license in engineering. The courses are for about thirty months at a cost of about $450. RCA and C.I.E. (Cleveland Institute of Electronics) are two companies that offer these courses. There are no schools teaching sound engineering at present. Cal adds this useful observation, "Each studio teaches their personnel different from another studio. Your best experience is picked up in the small studio and/or radio-TV stations where you have to do everything." The essence of making a success in this kind of engineering is the same as in other careers, your readiness to contribute. You'll need keen hearing, excellent health, and social skills.

Front Men

The front man chooses to work as number one assistant to the star: he warms up the crowd, leads the band, sings harmony with the star. Some of the best front men in the business are: Bill Phillips (with Johnny Wright and Kitty Wells); Jimmy Gately (Bill Anderson); Bobby Sykes (Marty Robbins); Blake Emmons (Jim Ed Brown). Jack Greene formerly fronted for

OTHERS WHO GET THE WORK OUT

Ernest Tubb. In general, the front man is the vanguard who builds the initial excitement for the star. He may be given administrative work by the star. His earnings are in ratio to those of his boss the star, and his, or her, liberality or lack of it; but many front men get by nicely and report that they enjoy their work.[1] Many stars fronted in their past. If you think you would be interested in joining a band and working up to front man, send a tape of your playing or singing to an established artist, with a note giving your correct age and telling about your background. If you're a minor, wait a while; many stars are skittish about employing minors, due to contractual difficulties. Note: before submitting a tape to a star, do like songwriters and arrangers do, namely, *know* what the star does. Probably a trumpet rendition of "Stars and Stripes Forever" would not turn on Bill Monroe or Roy Acuff to consider you as a possibility for their bands. The example is extreme, but the point is urgent: to sell your work, first know the market.

Promoters

The top pay in the business is here, particularly for idea men. The life is hard, fast-paced, everchanging. Paths of entry include radio and television, newspapers, magazines. This is how Wally Cochran, director of country and western promotion for RCA, Nashville, talks about his job: "There are people in the music industry who will tell you that the hardest job in the business is that of the promotion man. He catches it from all sides if a record doesn't sell, and if it does, everybody else claims to have made it a hit. Well, perhaps it is the hardest job, but my twenty-odd years spent in promotion have been great, and I wouldn't have it any other

---

[1] For a view of this work see Larry King, "The Grand Ole Opry," *Reader's Digest*, October, 1968, pp. 96-100.

way. You're caught up in an exciting world where something is always happening, and what is happening is people."

Secretaries

Correctly used, the term "secretary" denotes men and women who have passed qualifying tests offered by the National Secretaries Association, and similar organizations throughout the country. Persons so qualified should meet with no severe difficulty in placing themselves in the recording industry, but the top pay probably is found in offices in California and New York. Information about pay is limited, but salaries for secretaries in Nashville generally range between $300-$400 a month, and higher, depending on length of service, and the preparation of the worker.

Dorothy (Dot) Boyd, of RCA Nashville, explains that secretaries in the recording industry prepare paperwork for the A&R men before and after recording sessions, determine the correct song titles, publishers, and writers of the material the artist prepares (of great importance), and otherwise coordinates the many forms, regulations, and the like, used every day, every hour, in the business end of the music industry.

An approach for young people just out of high school and with general typing skill, some shorthand and filing skills, is to take a job doing stenographic or general clerical work. Salary and working conditions, in general, will match those in other businesses; local inquiry for updated information is suggested. Receptionist is another job open to younger people, especially females who are attractive and well groomed, and talented in taking and relaying messages. Reports indicate that work in such jobs nearly always is interesting and the workday passes quickly. Many times a job of this general type provides bread-and-butter money for an aspiring composer until he makes it with his music.

OTHERS WHO GET THE WORK OUT

Free-lance art, photography, writing

There are some opportunities for free-lancing in the various arts that are needed in recordings. If you think you would like to write the notes for the back of an album for a particular artist, submit a sample "liner" to the A&R man who produces the recordings of the star. He may give you a chance to write a liner. Usually the pay is $50, and you will be expected to attend at least one session. The experience is stimulating in many ways. For instance, just seeing and feeling how hard musicians work can energize a writer. At the sessions you will make contacts that could lead to the writing of bios (biographies), brochures, and publicity for performers. One thing leads to another. You can earn $3,000 a year in this writing, but, obviously, to live you'll need to do other kinds of writing too. Free-lance photographers and artists are often used in creating album covers and special materials. Ask an A&R man, whose work you know and like, for permission to leave with him samples of your work.

Conclusion

In a changing world with an increasing population and more leisure time, recorded music gives indication of growth potential. Uses for recorded sound hardly have been tapped. More sophisticated ways of recording are now under development. Thus there should be careers, careers, and more careers in the recording industry. Many years ago, Paul Heinecke, founder of Sesac, stated what now is becoming most evident in a time when over 200 people will fly from London to Nashville to attend a country music convention; and when it is only five hours from Nashville to Los Angeles: "Music is the common denominator . . . a communications instrument international in scope that knows no language barrier. Man's creative melodies provide the ideal setting for improved international understanding." This is all so true, whether the scale is regional, national, or international. Music now is the marvelous communicator, and recorded music may be shared equally well by all men.

If you have used this book, thought about yourself and your chances critically and carefully, the time to break into the recording business is now, not later. You will find opportunities for personal growth when you contribute as a professional to the advancement of recorded music. Such music aptly qualifies as a common denominator between people.

Appendix I
Questions the Professionals Don't Have Time to Answer

Here are questions that often are asked of professionals by those aspiring to make the recorded music scene. While most professionals do counsel with amateurs, their time always is in short supply. Commonly enough, many professionals are afraid of making a very involved situation too simple and easy. Here are some pertinent questions, some not covered elsewhere in this book, and a few that need reviewing because of their merit. The answers are not intended as the last, final word on the various subjects.

Q. Some stars seem conceited and high-hat toward the public, autograph seekers, and the like. Why?

A. Some may be the way you describe, since recording stars are drawn from a wide spectrum of humanity. We must say that our experiences with them have been the opposite. No doubt it requires a certain amount of ego to face up to a crowd or a studio mike. A person couldn't do it without a high degree of self-confidence. Stars have their off moments just like other people, and some autographer seekers can be insufferable.

Q. I write for my high school paper and tried to get an interview with ——— ——— (a noted recording star). He wouldn't see me.

A. This can happen, even to an amateur writer like you. We should make it clear that if you're going to try for a career as a

SO YOU WANT TO BE IN MUSIC!

free-lance writer specializing a little in music, you should expect a rocky road. You may be turned down for many interviews. Now and then a star may decline an interview because he has little use for publicity, or has been misquoted in the past. Interviews in print may turn out different from the way they were spoken. Meticulous attention should be given to arranging for your requested interview. A good place to start is the promotional office. It's a good idea to submit questions in advance. But you take your chances here, as in anything else.

Q. Why do some musicians prefer big, expensive cars?

A. They are people. Even Vance Packard couldn't dig up all the reasons why people buy automobiles. There are, however, some excellent reasons for the apparent preference of many artists and sidemen for late-model, high-powered cars. They are useful for carting around musical instruments, changes of clothing, folios of sheet music, and the like. Getting repair work done is a big problem for any car owner. Since a star never has much time, it's best for him to have a car that doesn't have to go to the garage often, a new one. Expensive cars are one sign of success. Not unlike other people, many stars grew up with dreams of owning a Cadillac. And many stars say that the public expects them to own costly automobiles.

Q. Why do so many stars travel in custom-built buses that even have color television?

A. The star's real money is not made from recordings, but from appearances at fairs, colleges, shopping-center dedications, political rallies, and the like. Nashville stars hit Canada as often as they do the South, the Midwest, or California. The trend favors bigger bands, too, six to a dozen, or more, traveling sidemen. A good average for a star and his company in a year is 100,000 miles of surface travel, often to points not reached by commercial airlines. So, a star finds it practical to have a $50,000 bus.

Q. I have talent as a singer, but am afraid of hecklers. Why are they that way?

A. This is a question that really suits a book on performing in public, but there could be some heckling of newcomers in recording studios. It's best to ignore the heckling. If you go on to perform in nightclubs, you'll learn how to deal with people who

QUESTIONS THE PROFESSIONALS DON'T HAVE TIME TO ANSWER

come just to entertain themselves by needling the entertainer.

Q. Where do you get ideas for songs?

A. Anywhere. John Loudermilk says, "The Good Lord gives you these ideas. You better be ready when they come."

Q. What about writing habits?

A. Some write well late at night, some in the morning, some afternoons. One of the most competent composers, Boudelaux Bryant (700 published songs), says it doesn't matter when you write, but you must write regularly and build up volume. However, other established songwriters say they write in spurts, do a lot of songs, and then take off for a while. Few credit the idea of writing only when the inspiration hits you. Many successful songwriters keep regular office hours. It's a business.

Q. I'm always reading about lawsuits involving composers, recording firms, music publishers, and others in the business. Why is this so?

A. Historians say that Americans are characterized by a proneness to litigation, getting a lawyer, and going to court. Another reason may be that lawsuits are news. Also, many of the lawsuits you read about never make it to court. There are many chances for misunderstanding in the business; many do not know anything about contracts and agreements.

Q. Do you believe an agent can help an amateur get into the business?

A. Maybe; maybe not. Agents must have a list of clients whose recordings sell, and who, accordingly, are in demand for appearances at good fees. Unless you're outstanding, you probably won't interest an agent who knows the business.

Q. I've been writing for five years and have had no acceptances. Am I right or am I wrong in suspecting that I ought to give up the songwriting urge?

A. Five years is a long time. You may be composing strictly for self-expression and may lack the commercial touch. We don't know, but you evidently have some other means of support. Quite a few songwriters have had their first hit in middle age.

Q. Why is there so much competition?

A. There are lots of people trying to get into the business, and a lot of them are very talented. This is known and accepted

SO YOU WANT TO BE IN MUSIC!

by every professional writer, artist, sideman, and A&R man in the business.

Q. I have read that many "insiders" resent newcomers, like composers or recording artists.

A. As in other fields, there may be a hazing period for beginners.

Q. What is the obligation of the sideman to the artist?

A. You've answered your question by your use of terms. The sideman functions as just that—an auxiliary player—to the artist, who is king.

A. I'm a loner, do I have to join so many associations?

B. There are two or three perspectives on this question. Take songwriting. Like other writing, it is begun in solitude, but writing has to be edited and polished, and this means working with other people. At this time in the growth of the recording industry, professional memberships are quite desirable. Mavericks and rebels occasionally make the grade in any field, but many more win by playing according to the rules that are widely accepted. Too, memberships in organizations give a feeling of professionalism that is worthwhile. So much in this business depends on your ability to work effectively with people that you need to participate in organizations and associations. In a sense, it's one way of learning how to deport yourself as an ethical member of a profession.

Q. What about union membership? Is it necessary? How old must you be? How do you join? What are the costs?

A. George Cooper, Jr., president of the Nashville local, American Federation of Musicians, says that membership is necessary. He added that he might be expected to make a statement like this, but explained that the union is ever on the job in matters of pay and working conditions. Other authorities back up Cooper's statement. Anyone over twenty-one may join. And anyone under twenty-one may join provided parents or guardians sign an agreement to that effect. Even minors under sixteen may become members under the same arrangement. For example, Hank Williams, Jr., became a union member when he was thirteen. Union dues are $25 a year, plus 2 percent of net earnings, from which contributions are made to the pension and welfare fund, which

QUESTIONS THE PROFESSIONALS DON'T HAVE TIME TO ANSWER

covers the $2,000 paid at death. Cooper further explained that the organization is not a strong-arm union, but uses arbitration wherever possible.

Q. There is much discussion of good taste in music, with some songs banned by radio stations. What is good taste?

A. Good taste, roughly, is what the majority of people will accept. Beethoven once was dismissed for lacking good taste. There are some underground songs that many people would not like. If you're going to be a professional in this business, we remind you that you will be seeking the widest possible audience. We suppose that which is banal and trite is the opposite of that which is excellent. Somebody has said, "Last year's corn ain't fresh this year." Many things are accepted quite casually now in songs that ten years ago would have been scandalous to many.

Q. There's real money in this business if you're good. Is that why the stars, writers and sidemen strive so hard?

A. Motivation differs from person to person, but for quite a few the money return is one way, at least, of keeping score on how well you play the game. There's no reason why people who excel in this business should be underpaid.

Appendix 2
Glossary of Professional Terms

The following is a glossary of terms that may need additional clarification. You may already know what the terms mean from having read the book. In addition, a few terms used by engineers and A&R men are explained.

Artist: the featured performer, the star, the name that sells the recording. The one out of whose royalties the recording company pays the musicians used in the sessions.

Band: in amateur circles, widely used to refer to country & western and rock instrumental groups; roughly comparable to a combo.

Big sound: a strong trend, in nearly all popular recorded music, toward the large instrumental group, exemplified in Danny Davis and the Nashville Brass, Ray Price and his thirty-piece traveling orchestra. Probably influenced by increasing sophistication of recording technology.

Bios: sometimes called handouts; brief stories about the careers of stars; not always reliable. Many stars now insist on more carefully prepared "publicity packages."

Board: recording console, where A&R men, engineers, and technicians work; where stars listen to the playback of a tape after a session. Later the scene of intensive work in editing and mixing in which many stars like to participate.

GLOSSARY OF PROFESSIONAL TERMS

Brighten: generally means to increase tempo slightly. "Put an edge on it."

Cancellation: the legal procedure used by a recording company holding a contract on a star who is not producing, or used by the latter if he loses confidence in the firm. Normally contracts are reviewed annually and renewed or not renewed by the recording company. The company customarily will not announce the dropping of an artist. Many stars—for instance, Loretta Lynn—have lifetime contracts with a recording company.

Catalogue: refers to both the composer and the music publisher, both of whom strive to build "a good catalogue" of songs that will retain appeal. These catalogues often are distributed gratis in large quantities to recording firms. They are respected by recorders because they contain words and music that have lasted. These catalogues also are distributed to arrangers, sidemen, and stars. The practice reflects an ancient merchandising technique developed by large, diverse firms, such as Sears, Roebuck, and others. The catalogue is a great convenience to all who make recordings, for not everything that is recorded is intended to be new or topical.

Chart: a listing of best-selling recordings, in the order of their popularity, in trade publications. Some radio stations and newspapers also compile charts. The term is also used to refer to arrangements used on a recording date.

Chart action: when a recording goes upward in the popularity charts. There are "regionals," or "territorials," or "nationals" in the charts, as well as more localized ones. When someone boasts, "My song is getting chart action," the clarifying question ought to be, "What chart or charts?"

Cold: uninspired, not excited. May refer to the attitude of either the artist or the sidemen, or both, toward the material they are to record. The A&R man and the leader must apply whatever arts and skills are at their command to get production from "cold" musicians. A term with related meaning is "hang up." Also means to begin a song with no instrumental introduction. In other words, the artist "takes it cold."

SO YOU WANT TO BE IN MUSIC!

Country: in popular terminology, it refers, Grant Turner says, to a style of music with a strong lyric and rhythmical melody. It is closely associated with "western." There is traditional country, middle-of-the-road country, and "big sound" country. A major idiom at present is country music that has been influenced by Canadian folk music.

Demo (demonstration recording): a relatively inexpensive (though not always) tape or acetate recording, used to demonstrate (pitch) a composition, or to show an artist's potential. Made in a large quantities by commercial songwriters. Often a composer puts his arrangements on demos. He does not get royalties from demos or from arrangements. They are given to music publishers, who listen to them, evaluate them, and then submit those with potential to the appropriate A&R producer. In some instances, the composer may personally carry the demo to the recording firm or the producer. The successful composer spends many more hours in studios making demos than the star spends in the recording studio. Many music publishers have their own elaborately equipped studios for making demos.

Employment for hire: service for a flat fee (no royalties), in arranging, writing album liners, or working as a sideman. Stipulated in agreement or contract.

Folio: song book, usually paper bound, 9 by 12 inches, and sold both by music publishers and local music stores. May contain a dozen or more songs, both words and music, of an individual composer, or a grouping of songs by many composers on one theme. Important sources of royalties for composers; their sales indicate that the market for sheet music is far from dormant. Usually contain the composer's best-selling "catalogue songs," as previously described. Folios are useful to amateur writers who want to study the form of commercial songs.

Head arrangement: usually, to be played by ear, or without fully written-out arrangement.

Infringement: abuse of copyright; plagiarism, or appropriation of another's material.

GLOSSARY OF PROFESSIONAL TERMS

Independent: composer or producer not regularly employed by a specific music publisher or recording company. Sometimes "freelance."

Label: the trademark or brand name of the manufacturer. Term is used to signify a particular company, for instance, the Columbia label, the Decca label, Epic label, Monument label, and so on.

Lead guitar: term used to distinguish a guitar playing fills from a guitar playing only rhythm (rhythm guitar). Usually amplified, in contrast to rhythm guitar.

Lead sheet: manuscript of a song showing lyric, melody, and chord captions.

Leader: may be thought of as the representative of the union; works with producer in getting the session accomplished; generally designated by A&R man. Union requires that sessions with six musicians or more must have a leader. Obviously, he must be a superior musician able to command the respect of other gifted musicians, and at the same time capable of working with the producer and other officials of the recording company. Chet Atkins, who started as a sideman, first won recognition from RCA when Steve Sholes noted that he had abilities as a natural leader.

License: legal permission, usually written, to perform or record a song. The *licensee* is the recording company (manufacturer); the *licensor* is the copyright owner or, possibly, his agent.

Lick: improvised musical phrase (instrumental), sometimes called a "fill."

Liner: sometimes "annotations," or notes, on the back of a dust jacket for an LP album. In Britain, known as "sleeve notes." They are important and valid parts of the total effort. Many stars, like George Hamilton IV and Johnny Cash write their own liner notes. Full liner notes are helpful to amateur songwriters.

Logging: tabulation system used by ASCAP, BMI, and others for determining the air play of compositions written by their members.

Mechanicals: royalties paid by recording amateurs on the sales

SO YOU WANT TO BE IN MUSIC!

of a recording. Usually two cents a single recording paid to the music publisher, who then usually pays the writer 50 percent or one cent. If royalties do not meet production expenses, no royalties can be paid, and the recording company absorbs the loss.

Mix: to blend sounds electronically.

Musicology: the historical and theoretical investigation and analysis of specific types of music.

Open-door policy: the practice of listening to all submitted tapes or demos, however poor. Many publishers and recording companies cannot afford this policy. The amateur needs to realize that it is quite expensive and rarely, if ever, produces anything for either publisher or recorder.

Overdub: sometimes "dub in"; to add additional sound, music, or voice to a recording after the session. Harmony often is overdubbed. A daily part of the recording music business, due to eight- and sixteen-track recording machines.

Pickup musicians: pickers hired locally by traveling shows. These shows are often called "package shows," meaning they involve a number of performers.

PR: public relations, now increasingly sharp in the industry.

Publication (regular): the printing and marketing of a musical composition by an established music publisher.

Release: that portion of a song following the bridge (or middle part of the chorus). In a song following the *aaba* form, the final *a* section is the release. Also signifies the date a new recording is available to producers. Young, or new, songwriters and performers must learn that plugging a recording before it is available, or plugging it too soon, or too late, is bad business. It is also considered bad business to announce what your new recording will be before it can be bought by the consumers. You might get covered, that is, someone else might bring out their version of your song ahead of your release date. Songs often are recorded under strict secrecy to protect against this.

GLOSSARY OF PROFESSIONAL TERMS

Royalty statements: a semiannual itemized account of earnings. Sent to a writer from the music publisher; or to a recording artist from the recording company.

Session: the period during which recording is done. An electronic and human effort to tape musical sound, 3 hours.

Sideman: one who backs up the artist.

Song poem: No such entity exists under copyright law or in the practice of the music business, though the term is widely used by song sharks, and some naive amateurs. The law states that a song is a musical composition, or words with music; a poem cannot be a commercial song, under copyright law.

Spooks: cruel term for those who badger and pester professionals.

Star: Does not strictly belong in this book, but generally applied to those who make it in the recording scene and then choose to perform in public, with all which that entails—costumes, fan clubs, publicity, etc.

Take: refers to the taping of a specific run-through of a number. First attempt is "take 1," second is "take 2," and so on, until the final acceptable attempt, which is called "the take." The latter generally indicates a consensus of approval from producer and artist, influenced by the opinions of the engineers and sidemen ("How many *takes* were needed to record that song?" "We got it in four takes.").

Track: On multiple-head recorders, one of the recording lanes. Mono (monaural), stereo, 3, 4, 8, 16, etc. With multiple tracks, parts may be changed, added later, etc., simply by using an open track—one, as yet unused.

Turn: generally, a surprise ending; can be a turn on an old folk expression (What you don't know hurts you, for example).

Vamp: instrumental prelude or succession of chords that establishes a rhythm. "Vamp till ready" means to repeat the vamp over and over again until the artist is ready to sing and musicians are

SO YOU WANT TO BE IN MUSIC!

ready to play. Someone said that "Stardust" may have been inspired by a vamp. A vamp is often helpful in overcoming the musicians' problem of being cold.

Vanity publication: anything a writer has printed or published at his own expense ("the ego trade").

Appendix 3
The "Nashville Shorthand"

The place was RCA's Studio A on 17th Avenue, South, in the heart of Nashville's "Record Row," a compact, approximately four-block-square area of Music City, U.S.A. David Cobb, veteran WSM announcer, once told one of the authors of this handbook, "I came up with 'Music City, U.S.A.' in 1946, before the city fathers were the slightest bit interested in music. I wish I had thought to copyright it." The Grand Ole Opry was the magnet that drew the country and western talent, or the musicians who could play and sing country and western, among them a young guitarist named Chet Atkins, who now presides over RCA's studios.

Studio A was visited after a recording session one afternoon. It is one of the largest recording studios in the United States and can easily hold a hundred musicians. It is not "dead," not totally soundproofed, for Chet had it designed that way; he believes that musicians would be depressed by dead silence. Even after a session a vacant recording studio has a presence, a tingle, that you feel.

At least that was how it was in Studio A, as you looked around and saw empty paper cups, pop bottles, milk cartons, drinking straws, portions of sandwiches, and other indications that men and women had worked here three or four hours earlier. Your attention was attracted to envelopes and slips of paper here and there, on which numbers were inscribed. These numbers constitute the "Nashville Shorthand," a quick and easy way to transcribe the eight intervals in an octave.

In the notation the 3 x's indicate that the song is in three-quarter time. In this example, the one chord is E^b if performed in the same key as the sheet music. However, the song can be played in any key, using the shorthand

WINGS OF A DOVE
3 x's

E 1111 4444
  5555 1111
  1111 4444
  1155 1-411

CHO.
  1111 4444
  1155 1-411

method, as no key is referred to in the notation. The pickup notes are not given in the shorthand version except at the end of the verse leading into the chorus.

Simply expressed, the key in which you are playing becomes number 1 in this shorthand, and the succeeding numbers, up to 7, are the intervals in the octave. The eighth interval is not numbered 8, because it is the same as the 1 chord—the major, or tonic, key of the song. For example, if you are playing a song in the key of C, C is the 1 chord, D:2; E:3; F:4; G:5; A:6; B:7; and C again is the 1.

A value of this system is that it is very simple to transpose if the need arises. Perhaps you wish to do the same song in the key of D. Then D becomes the 1 chord, E the 2 chord, and so on up the scale.

A second value is that rather lengthy songs can be written in a small space. Of course, the melody of the song is not transcribed in this manner, or even suggested. Chord patterns can fit many different songs. By the basic chord pattern can be written down in a hurry. In a recording situation, the sidemen make up these miniature charts in a matter of minutes by listening to the recording artist run through a song, or by listening to a demo.

This shorthand, according to Junior Huskey, an expert in its use, favors the improvisation that is one of the qualities of the Nashville Sound. If there is difference of opinion as to which chords will be used in a particular recording, it is settled at the time the shorthand charts are written down in the last few minutes before a recording is made. This transcription, right on the recording date, allows for maximum flexibility. Junior Huskey stated, "With a system like this, you don't have to be a player piano. You can transpose as fast as you can write. The practice goes back as far as Beethoven, in reality." Even so, it is particularly useful in the recording studio situation, where time is of the essence.

Some years ago, a writer for the *Saturday Evening Post* declared in an article that Nashville musicians did not read music but that they played by a code. He obviously had seen examples of the Nashville Shorthand.

Reading List

Here are selected readings that will be stimulating to you in many ways. For instance, these readings will further illustrate the present healthy exchange between the various kinds of popular music. Of course no professional musician or writer can master the many varieties of musical expression, but an awareness of many kinds is one way of finding new ideas and learning new techniques.

1. *Periodicals*

Billboard, Cash Box, Record World, Variety, and a few other trade publications, are "must" reading. In addition, the publications' annual directories and various special issues are packed with colorful data that show the international scope of the recording business. *Country Song Roundup,* now in its twenty-first year, primarily is a fan publication, but regularly carries long taped interviews plus lyrics of best-selling songs, some of them pop. It prints many fan letters that give insight into the consumer, his likes and dislikes, and his general psychology. The *New Yorker* magazine often covers music, live and recorded, usually jazz and rock, but sometimes country and western, pop, and folk. *Time, Life, Look, Newsweek, Esquire,* and others regularly consider musical developments.

2. *Newspapers*

The Sunday edition of the *New York Times,* its amusement and entertainment section and Magazine, probably is the one best nontechnical source for following music trends.

3. *Books*

Among the welter of books about rock, these rank as the most painstaking, interesting, and free from specialized language: John Gabree, *The World of Rock* (Greenwich, Conn.: Fawcett World,

SO YOU WANT TO BE IN MUSIC!

1968); Ralph J. Gleason, *The Jefferson Airplane and the San Francisco Sound* (Ballantine Books, 1969). Jonathan Eisen has edited the thick anthology entitled *The Age of Rock* (Vintage, 1969), which is addressed to "Sounds of the American Cultural Revolution." There are chapters on The Beatles, Bob Dylan, folk music, protest music, psychedelia, San Francisco, Nashville, New York, and Detroit.

Far too many books on The Beatles have been quickly published. Eventually something substantial about them will appear, hopefully.

One of the best works of its kind is Red O'Donnell's *Chet Atkins* (Athens Music Company, 1967). The student will also want to consult Red's writings on "Music City" in the *Nashville Banner*.

Other books that may interest you include: Ross Lee Finney, *The Game of Harmony* (New York: Harcourt, 1947), a standard work written with contagious enthusiasm; Linnell Gentry, *A History and Encyclopedia of Country, Western and Gospel Music*, second edition (Nashville: Clairmont Corp., 1969), an indispensable book which reprints seventy-six articles from a variety of sources and gives bios of hundreds of people working in country and western, and gospel. Leston Huntley, *The Language of the Music Business* (Nashville: Del Capo Publications, 1965), limited edition of 400 copies, most useful but hard to secure; Bill C. Malone, *Country Music, U.S.A.: A Fifty-Year History* (Austin, Texas: University of Texas Press, 1968), an informative work, originally a Ph.D. dissertation published for the American Folklore Society; Thurston Moore, ed., *The Country Music Who's Who* (Denver; 1966); Robert Shelton and Burt Goldblatt, *The Country Music Story: A Picture History of Country and Western Music* (Indianapolis; Bobbs-Merrill, 1966), a careful work devoid of special pleading; Sidney Shemel and M. William Krasilovsky, edited by Paul Ackerman, *This Business of Music* (New York: *Billboard*, 1964), the authority on contracts, copyright, and international aspects of music, detailed and comprehensive, but technical.

Three books by Tom Wolfe are recommended to those who want to dig a little into the contemporary setting in which music is almost a way of life: *The Pump House Gang* (New York: Farrar, Straus & Giroux, 1968); *The Electric Kool-Aid Acid Test* (F, S & G,

READING LIST

1968); *The Kandy-Kolored Tangerine-Flake Streamline Baby* (Noonday; F, S & G, 1969).

4. *Other Sources of Information*

Experience suggests that amateurs often want suggestions about developing their own sources of information. Here then are some possible sources:

Two monthly publications, both published in Nashville, regularly chronicle musical happenings there. One is *Music City News*, a monthly tabloid, fan-oriented, covering country and western and gospel. Another is the monthly magazine *Nashville*, a general publication that gives attention to business aspects of music, but also reports on outstanding music personalities from time to time.

Various publications of ASCAP, BMI, Sesac and brochures of major publishers and recorders are available usually gratis to a bona fide student by writing the New York offices. Write American Music Conference, 332 South Michigan Avenue, Chicago, Illinois, for a list of publications with prices. A visit to the library of the Country Music Hall of Fame and Museum in Nashville may turn up many other sources of information. While there, learn about the work of the Country Music Association, which operates the institution.

INDEX

Acuff, Roy, 63
Acuff-Rose, 63
Affluent Society, The (Galbraith), 111
AFTRA, 17
Alcohol, and musicians, 25
Alpert, Herb, 95
American Federation of Musicians, 17, 133-37
American Music Conference, 21, 23, 45
Anderson, Bill, 89, 95
Anderson, Liz, 42
Anka, Paul, 84
A&R men, 141-44
Appearances, personal, 89
Apprenticeship, 49-50, 68
Arnold, Eddy, 53
Arrangers, 144
ASCAP, 17
Atkins, Chet, 20, 25, 84, 106, 118, 121-22, 124

Baez, Joan, 19
Bare, Bobby, 100
Barnum, P. T., 63
Berlin, Irving, 76
Better Business Bureau, 61
"Blue Moon of Kentucky," 96
BMI, 17
Boone, Pat, 50
"Boots," 41, 46
"Both Sides Now," 90

Bowen, Jimmy, 141
Bowman, Don, 106
Bradley, Owen, 77, 105
Break, the Big, 41

Careers, musical
 and amateur competition, 23
 sidemen, 129-38
 songwriting, 57-92
 and supporting jobs, 139-50
"Carroll County Accident," 90
Cash, Johnny, 20, 89, 96
Catch-22 (Heller), 104
"Cause I Love You," 109-10
Charles, Ray, 20
"Chit Akins, Make Me a Star," 106
Clement, Jack, 123
Coben, Cy, 70
Cochran, Wally, 147-48
Collins, Judy, 90
"Come-on," the, 61
Composition, musical
 definition of, 54, 71-72
Contracts
 long-term, 53
 songwriting, 72
Copyright, 70-75
 Canadian, 71
 European, 73
 law, 70-71
 length of, 72

171

Copyright—cont'd
  reform of, 72-73
  registration, 73
Co-writer fallacy, 77, 81

Darrell, Johnny, 91
Davis, Danny, 68
Day, Doris, 60
Detroit Sound, 98-99
Disc jockey, 108-9
Discipline, of performer, 54-55
DJ. See disc jockey
Dropouts, 33
Dropping out
  in general, 36-38
  of school, 33-36
Drugs, and musicians, 25
Dylan, Bob, 37

Education, for musicians, 35-36
Egbert, Marion S., 23
Emery, Ralph, 19, 42
Engineers, 145-46
Enjoyment in music, 23
Evaluation of songs, 66
Experience, music
  acquiring, 49
  at home, 48-49
  value of, 43, 45
  vicarious, 51

Fans, performer's relationship
  with, 54
Fee, flat, 62-63
Feliciano, Jose, 20
Ferguson, Bob, 90, 119
"Fly Me to the Moon," 18
Foster, Fred, 77
Free-lancing, 149

Galbraith, John Kenneth, 111

Garland, Judy, 45
Gleason, Ralph J., 100
Goals, of professional, 25, 49, 50-51
Gold records, 83
Gordy, Berry, Jr., 98, 107
Grand Ole Opry House, 20
"Green, Green Grass of Home," 91
Gretsch guitars, 122
Guitar boom, 122

Haggard, Merle, 89
Hall, Tom T., 37
Hamilton, George, IV, 43
"Harper Valley PTA," 37
Harrison, George, 122
Hartford, John, 58
Heinecke, Paul, 149
Heller, Joe, 104
Hit song, definition of, 83
"Honey," 144
Howard, Harlan, 26, 47, 85
Husky, Ferlin, 50

Improvisation, 25
"In the Ghetto," 97
Industry. See recording industry
Interviews, 80

Jarvis, Felton, 142
Jarvis, Mary Lynch, 79
Jingles, 135
Jobs, nonperforming, 139-50
  accountants, 139-40
  advance men, 140
  agents, 140
  arrangers, 144
  artists, 149
  contractors, 145
  engineers, 145

INDEX

Jobs—*cont'd*
  front men, 146
  photographers, 149
  secretaries, 148
  writers, 149
Jones, Tom, 91
Jordanaires, 129

Kerr, Anita, 144
Kershaw, Doug, 89
King, Pee Wee, 62-63
"King of the Road," 89

Labels, recording
  major, 105
  importance of, to artist, 107-8
Lead sheets, 60
Lee, Peggy, 84, 109
Lewis, Jerry Lee, 96
Los Angeles, as music center, 109
Losers, 39, 62
Loudermilk, John D., 85

McCartney, Paul, 58
McCluskey, Bob, 77
McCuen, Brad, 63, 80
MacDonald, John D., 54
McKuen, Rod, 89
Malloy, Jim, 143
Material
  commercial, 82
  selection of, 84
Mechanical rights, 84-85
Memphis Sound, 96-97, 110
Mercer, Johnny, 76, 109
Miller, Roger, 89
Moog synthesizer, 130-31
Motown, 98
Music
  amateur, 97
  consumer market for, 18
  ethics, 23
  functions of, 20-21
  as profession, 23
  semiprofessional, 23
Music, recorded
  as common denominator, 150
  importance of, 38, 55, 92
  opportunities in, 55
  scope of, 18, 20-21
  sociology of, 33
  teen-age, 34
"My Happiness," 96

NARAS, 17, 72-73
Newbury, Mickey, 68
New York
  music publishers, 77
  Sound, 89

"Once a Day," 43
Open-door policy, 85
Opry, Grand Ole, 63
Orbison, Roy, 96
Ortega, Palito, 20
"Over the Rainbow," 45

Pay, union
  for network and video tape shows, 136
  per session, 133-34
  for sidemen, 133-35
  in supporting jobs, 139
Perkins, Carl, 96
Personal records, importance of, 80
Phillips, Sam, 96
Phonograph, invention of, 19
Presley, Elvis, 95
Preston, Frances, 70, 80, 138
Pride, Charlie, 42
Producers. See A&R men.
Professional musician

Professional musician—cont'd
  definition of, 23
  and equipment expenditure, 53
  experience, 45
  health hazards of, 53
  policies of, toward amateurs, 105
  preparation of, 25
  personality traits of, 24, 27-29
  and studio work, 87
Public domain, 72
Publisher, music
  choice of, 77-78
  legitimate, 59, 76
  and unsolicited material, 61
  vanity, 59-64
Purcell, Bill, 25
Putman, Claude T., Jr., 90

Radio
  developments in, 19
  stations, 21
Randolph, Boots, 137-38
Readiness, for career, 49
Recording
  benefits of, to career, 42
  custom, 101
  demonstration, 61
Recording companies
  foreign, 18-19
  major-label, 105-10
Recording industry
  changes in, 19, 34, 57, 112
  distortion of, in movies, 39
  economics of, 111
  international aspects of, 18-19
  size of, 17-18
Recordings
  cost of, 114
  distribution of, 103-4
  growth potential of, 149
  hit, 83
  promotion of, 102
  returns from, direct, 115
  returns from, indirect, 116
  sales of, 18
  technology of, 58
Reed, Jerry, 91
Reeves, Mary, 85
Rejections, 85-86
Ritter, Tex, 42, 109
Rolling Stones, The, 53
Rose, Fred, 63
Ross, Diana, 99
Royalties
  for composers or songwriters, 88
  and general economics, 111
  limitations of, 53
  from million-seller recordings, 37
  for recording artist or star, 85

Sainte-Marie, Buffy, 20
Salesmanship, 79
San Francisco bands, 100
Sayers, Peter, 53
Scrapbooks and records, 43
Scruggs, Earl, 98
Self-evaluation, 65
Sesac, 17
Session, recording, 113, 124-26
Sharks, song, 59
Shearing, George, 26
Sholes, Steve, 97
Sidemen, studio, 129-38
  earnings of, 129-30
  working conditions, 129
Simon and Garfunkel, 58
Sinatra, Frank, Jr., 41
Sinatra, Nancy, 41, 46
Smith, Connie, 43, 95, 96
Snow, Hank, 68

INDEX

Songs
    cancelling effect of, 68
    catalogue, 88
    commercial, definition of, 57; qualities of, 65
    as compositions, 68
    evaluation of, 69
    "good," definition of, 65
    melodic trend in, 69
    requirements of, for recording, 68-69
    salability of, 67
    selection of, for recording, 82
    structure of, 67
    submission of, 77-81
Songwriters (composers)
    earnings, 89
    professional, number of, 88
Songwriting
    by contract, 75
    college preparation for, 47
    getting experience in, 48
    getting a start in, 47
Sound
    Detroit, 99
    Nashville, 118-21
    distinctive, in specific area, 120-21
Spector, Phil, 103
"Spooks," 80
Spores, Ronald, 67
Stewart, Redd, 63
Stevens, Ray, 25
Stewart, Jimmy, 109

Studio visits, 22, 123
Style, developing your own, 53
Success, overnight, 138
Superstars, 52

Talbot, Joe, 68-69
Tapes, unsolicited, 85
Technology, 58
Teen market, 114
"Tennessee Waltz, The," 63
Thomas, Carla, 109-10
Timing, 43, 45-46
Tin Pan Alley, 58

Union. *See* American Federation of Musicians

Van Heusen, Jimmy, 109

Wagoner, Porter, 127
Whaley, Cecil, 118
Wheeler, Billy Edd, 88
"White Christmas," 76
"Wildflowers," 90
"Wildwood Flower," 20
Williams, Hank, Jr., 42
Williams, Lawton, 72
Williams, Roger, 26
Wilson, Norro, 68
"Wings of a Dove," 90
Winston, Ken, 48-49
Winston, Nat T., Jr., 97
Wolfe, Tom, 103
WSM, 20, 63